INTERIOR
affairs

INTERIOR
affairs

—— • ——

ALEX DAVIDSON

THE DECORATIVE ARTS
IN PAINTWORK

WARD LOCK

For Roger and Flavia

and all students, past, present
and future, attending the Decorative
Arts Course at the City and
Guilds College of Art,
Kennington.

First published in Great Britain in
paperback in 1989 by Ward Lock Limited.
New Edition 1991.

Photographs by Mike Henton
Drawings by Pam Corfield

Phototypeset in 11/12pt Garamond Original
by Tradespools Ltd., Frome, Somerset

Printed in Hong Kong by
Colorcraft Ltd.

British Library Cataloguing in Publication Data
Davidson, Alex
Interior affairs
I. Interior decoration–Amateur's manuals
I. Title
643'.7 TH8026

ISBN 0 7063 7012 0

Acknowledgments

To Margret, Louise and Richard for their tuition and enthusiasm, which fired my studies.
My warmest thanks and gratitude to Phillipa and Chloe, Alidad and Mariam, Sally and
Rupert, Mary Ann and Richard, the friends and patrons of my beginnings.
To Noeleen, a special thanks for the use of the library at Ottershaw, along with the
numerous glasses of refreshments.
For all the hard work, long hours and frustrations dealt with patiently and with care by
Mike the lens, Pam the pen, Kate's copy-typing and Georgina's fine brush-work.
A sincere thanks to Geoff, whose quiet understanding when the going was tough
pulled me through.
Most of all, for his total support and dedication to my work, I wish to thank Michel;
an anchor at home-base when my head reached too far into the clouds. For his help
through the midnight hours when the type-writer started to come to life in conflict with my
eyelids.
For all my clients that never questioned why or how, letting me loose to experiment in
their homes.
I thank you.

CONTENTS

FOREWORD

It has been my aim within the pages that follow, to keep the text, the terminology and methods used in my work as a decorative artist, as uncomplicated as possible. For the beginner, simplicity is the key word.

There is no mystery surrounding the world of decorative paint-work. However, in the past, doors have stayed locked, and jealously guarded techniques have gone to the grave with their creators for the want of a trusty apprentice or the keeping and handing down of notes. As a result, wonderful finishes by craftsmen of great skill and imagination are lost to us for ever.

Success with the different techniques described here will probably be a slow process. Do not be put off if your first attempts are poor. A marble effect that veers towards zebra stripes is not such a bad thing, and who knows, it may look more attractive than the marbling you had first planned. My own first attempts at rag-rolling certainly had a lunar-landscape look about them. The old saying about practice making perfect certainly applies here.

Treat the book as a step by step guide/recipe book and your work should be easier to accomplish. The drawings and photographs give an idea of how to use the different materials and mediums, together with an insight into what the finished look can achieve in the home. There are guidelines to follow if you have a problem, and tips on saving time and money.

Once your confidence has grown, and you have taken the criticism along with the applause, do experiment. Play as much as you can with colours, materials and different modes of application. With fantasy at the fingertips, let your imagination run riot.

An exotic combination of colours turn this entrance hall into an Aladdin's Cave. Gun-metal grey on the ceiling and walls has been given an oil glaze in both herring-bone and bagging techniques. The door architrave, marbled to a sodalite blue, creates a perfect foil for the water resist treatment of malachite. Glittering high-lights of poor man's gold, in just the right proportion, lift the subterranean depths to a sheer, magical level.

INTRODUCTION

Man's first fire, at the heart of his home, could be described as the forerunner of the kitchen we know today. It was in the early kitchen that man took the first steps towards becoming a decorative artist. Using the scorched earth, charred wood, animal fats and bones produced by the fire, he created decorative images to enliven the walls that surrounded him, to please himself, to please his gods and to illustrate stories for his children. The concepts of this prehistoric man are still employed by us today. If we look back into any period of history, the decorative materials and the reasons for their being put into practice are still the same.

The rise and fall of civilizations, with their own cultures and fashions, have left us a legacy of inventiveness of staggering proportions in the field of decorative arts – from simplicity to complexity, from pure form to stylization and abstract translations of nature's work – giving us a veritable jigsaw puzzle that covers the earth.

Every museum houses a wealth of these stories and at times, on inspection, it is not difficult to trace a decorative motif through the ages to the present day. The design on a Byzantine pot can be found on a bishop's cope in the fifteenth century, on a French silk of the eighteenth century, and on a kitchen tile today.

The techniques described in this book are based on traditional methods and materials, artist's licence being used in areas where cost and time prohibit the use of the old, well-tested ways. New materials appear on the market all the time. As science develops these, it is left to the artist to think once more and create original modes of application.

W. Sutherland, in his book *The Grainer, Marbler and Signwriters Assistant* (published by William Hatton in 1854) said: 'The pupil will find as he goes on (if he is in earnest) that new ideas will spring up, and new methods will be suggested to him by accidental circumstances, which may possibly be better than some that are set down in this book, and why not? I do not presume to set any limit to genius; I merely tell him how I do them, and I have had twenty years experience.'

1 PREPARATION OF SURFACES

The following applies for techniques in this book – walls, furniture and *objets d'art* – unless otherwise stated at the beginning of the chapter.

The surface being decorated must be prepared to a high standard. It is no good using a marble effect or a tortoiseshell finish as a cosmetic cover-up for a poor surface. Hard work and elbow grease are needed before the powder and paint that face the outside world are applied. Cracks in plaster *do* have to be filled and sanded down, holes in woodwork made good, and all new surfaces (such as bare plaster and raw timber) sealed, before layers of colour are applied and worked in the technique of your choice.

If you do not have the time, or the inclination, to do the preparatory work yourself, make sure the painter doing the work understands exactly what finish is required by giving him the relevant instructions. It is a great pity to start glazing a wall, only to discover that it has been inadequately covered by the base coat. When the glaze sinks in, leaving large dark patches, you can do nothing about it except wipe all the glaze off and start the preparation again.

For techniques such as marbling and tortoise-shell, it is very important to use the correct base colour and this is specified in each section. For some other techniques, colour mixes are suggested. You should refer to the relevant section for advice on colour before starting the preparatory work.

New plaster
Whatever the paint, it will not adhere to the walls properly if there is any moisture retention, so always allow time for new plaster to dry out.
1   Apply one coat of sealer (available with a special base to stop salts and fungi appearing on the surface paintwork).
2   One coat (thinned if necessary) of flat white, oil paint or mid-sheen, oil-based paint.
3   Rub over lightly with a fine sandpaper.
4   One coat of mid-sheen, oil-based paint.
5   Rub over lightly with a fine sandpaper.
6   Final coat of mid-sheen, oil-based paint.

Old plaster (with paint over the top)
The walls should be washed down with cleaning agent, which takes away dust and grime and also helps to key in the surface so that the following coats of paint adhere.

Any deep cracks or holes should be filled in with an all-purpose filler. These will need quite some time to dry out. Do not worry about the surface being slightly rough, as a fine filler is used to finish off. This fine filler is best used on small cracks, and as a finish to the larger cracks once they have been filled and left to dry out. To save time: using a damp-dry household sponge five minutes or so after filling, gently wipe over the filled area until smooth. Sanding down can then be kept to a minimum.

1 If the areas filled are larger than 3 cm (1 in) square, it is advisable that they be sealed with a sealer or a thinned emulsion paint. This helps prevent the oil-based paint sinking into the porous surface.
2 One coat (thinned if necessary) of flat white, oil paint, or mid-sheen, oil-based paint.
3 Rub over lightly with fine sandpaper.
4 One coat of mid-sheen, oil-based paint.
5 Final coat of mid-sheen, oil-based paint.

Walls with a poor surface

If your walls are in very poor condition, and have been filled time and time again, you will achieve a better decorative finish if you line the walls before painting. Cracks still have to be filled and the surface made as smooth and as clean as possible. Then prepare the walls with a wash down with sugar soap or washing soda dissolved in hot water. Size the wall the day before the lining-paper is to be hung, following the manufacturer's instructions for mixing the wallpaper paste.

A good quality 800 grade lining paper will have enough body to cover cracks without their being clearly defined. Allow the paper to dry out thoroughly before applying the first coat of paint.

1 One coat of thinned down emulsion paint: 10 per cent clean water to paint. This stops any woolliness in the paper showing up, and seals the porous surface.
2 One coat of flat white, oil paint (thinned if necessary), or a coat of mid-sheen, oil-based paint.
3 Rub over lightly with fine sandpaper.
4 One coat of mid-sheen, oil-based paint.
5 Rub over lightly with a fine sandpaper.
6 Final coat of mid-sheen, oil-based paint.

To save time, a roller can be used for the first and second coats. A definite orange-peel look appears when the paint has been rollered onto a wall, which can hold traces of glaze. Therefore, although the top two coats can also be applied with a roller, they must always be brushed out to rid the surface of any small pit marks.

New woodwork (softwood)

1 All woodwork must be sanded down; nail holes filled and made flush with the surface.
2 Any knots in the wood should be given two light coats of shellac knotting. This prevents the resin in the wood from seeping through and splitting the new layers of paint. Some softwoods have few, others many. It is advisable to treat them all, no matter how small. Once done, the knotting should be left to dry.
3 Apply a coat of primer/sealer. The tree that your wood came from left the forest a long time ago, and by the time you buy it, will be ready for a good drink. This is where the primer/sealer comes into its own. Sinking right into the grain of the wood, it stops further coats doing the same.
4 Rub over lightly with fine sandpaper to remove any hairiness that the wood has developed whilst having its drink.
5 One coat of undercoat.

6 Rub over lightly with fine cabinet paper.
7 One coat of mid-sheen, oil-based paint.
8 Rub over lightly with fine cabinet paper.
9 Final top coat of mid-sheen, oil-based paint.

New woodwork (hardwood)

Unlike the softwoods, the grain of hardwood is very difficult to penetrate. An ordinary primer/sealer will work to a certain extent but not as well as an aluminium wood primer. The fine consistency of this primer is readily absorbed into the grain of the wood and gives a smooth easy surface to work on.

1 One coat of aluminium wood primer.
2 One coat of undercoat (thinned slightly), and allowed to dry.
3 Lightly sand down with wet and dry paper. This is better than fine sandpaper, as too coarse a sanding on the fine grain of hardwood will soon remove the primer.
4 One coat of mid-sheen, oil-based paint.
5 Lightly sand down with wet and dry paper.
6 Final coat of mid-sheen, oil-based paint.

Remember to give all the coats of paint time to dry out. Atmospheric conditions play a vital role in the performance of these painted finishes. Too damp an atmosphere and delays are inevitable. Heat and moisture combined, and the paint stays sticky to the touch longer. If you are not sure whether the surface is ready to take the next coat of paint, leave it overnight or possibly for a whole day. It would be a shame to spoil your chances of having a first-class job through impatience.

Preparation for metal

If the metal has never been painted before, then a good rubbing over with fine wire wool should be enough to clean the surface ready to paint.

Red oxide or grey metal primer are available in both tins and spray containers. For small objects, a spray saves time and is economical. For larger pieces, the tinned paint is less expensive but needs time to dry out, overnight in some cases. Depending on the technique to be employed as decoration on the metal, your paints can be sprayed or brushed on.

In preparation for an oil glaze, the following procedure will be necessary.

1 One coat of metal primer.
2 One coat of flat oil-based paint.
3 Lightly sand over when previous coat is dry.
4 One coat of mid-sheen, oil-based paint.
5 Lightly sand over when previous coat is dry.
6 Final coat of mid-sheen, oil-based paint.

Most metal objects, except *objets d'art*, will be required to take quite a lot of wear or strain, so it will be necessary to apply a good quality protective varnish to the area decorated.

2 OIL GLAZE TECHNIQUES

For many centuries, painters have used glazes in their work. The great artists, whose glazing palettes produced light and depths of incomparable beauty and subtlety, used them most advantageously between the sixteenth and eighteenth centuries. Black grapes bloomed with delicate lavenders; silk taffeta robes on being highlighted looked frost laden; brush strokes of genius to be marvelled at and envied.

Decorative painters learnt much from the great artists and soon adapted glazing techniques for their own work. Furniture of the French court was blushed with the palest of pastel colours, enhancing shape and form alike.

A glaze is a transparent layer of colour (pure pigment suspended in a clear medium) layed thinly over an opaque surface. It can be built up over and over again to create such depths that the eye of the beholder is tricked into believing a flat surface has more than one dimension.

With proper use, a glaze can transform quite a small area into one with a feeling of great space. A room with a cold northern light can become a Caribbean carnival of warmth. A matt finish will give peace and tranquility, while a glossy surface has a reflective value that mirrors furniture and surroundings into infinity.

For the most part, it is easier to buy ready-made oil glaze, known as scumble glaze. There are quite a few on the market, ranging from a fine wax like substance to darkest treacle and honey mixtures (see list of suppliers, pages 124–5). Alternatively, you can make your own.

Home-made glazing liquid

500 ml (1 pt) pure turpentine
300 ml (12 fl oz) boiled linseed oil
200 ml (8 fl oz) oil driers
1 tablespoon whiting
balloon whisk
polythene container

Mix all the ingredients together with a balloon whisk until the mixture becomes light and smooth. It can be stored for a short time, but does develop a skin after being exposed to the air.

If you are taking up a career in the decorative arts, and will often be using scumble glaze, an easy way to produce greater quantities without the elbow strain, is to mix all the ingredients in a kitchen blender. An inexpensive one could be kept just for this. (A blender used for mixing glaze should not be used again for any kind of food.)

Notes on mixing and using oil glazes

This glaze mixture differs from the commercial, tinned variety, by not having to be thinned down for application.

Using artists' oil paint, mix the colour of your choice in a small amount of turpentine if using the home-made glaze; or in a little of the scumble glaze. Do this in a separate container as you will have more control over mixing the colour.

You can now add this to the basic glaze in small amounts, stirring continuously until mixed.

The glaze should be mixed the day before you need it. This allows the mediums to become properly amalgamated and clarified, which improves the brushing qualities of the glaze.

You should always keep the room you are working in free from dust, dogs, cats and children; and even your next-door neighbour. Until the surface is dry, it must remain untouched, as it is very difficult to re-touch scuff marks once the glaze has been applied. The smallest finger-mark can ruin a stippled wall. The swish of a dog's tail means the whole wall has to be taken back to the base coat and started again. However, certain techniques, such as ragging, bagging and clouding, do not show discrepancies as much, in which case there is always a possibility that remedial glaze surgery using a fine paint-brush could do the trick.

Glaze gives off fumes, so some of the windows will have to be open while you are working in the room. Dust will blow in and adhere to the wet surface of the glaze, but this should be minimal if your windows are not open fully. If carpets have been left down in the room, do not take up your dust sheets and vacuum around the room until you have sealed the glazed surface with a light varnish. Let them stay down until completion of all the work.

Atmospheric conditions are all important. Oil glaze dries slowly; in good conditions twelve hours is the minimum length of time required. The surface may be touch-dry after six hours, once the white spirits evaporates, but oil paint dries slowly. On those damp days of winter forty-eight hours may be needed.

Breathing a sigh of relief that no damage has been done, check in every corner of the room to see if there are any runs or drips. Corners tend to retain more glaze than walls and may bear the marks of small rivulets. Using a fine artists' paintbrush, blend them in with light, fanning movements from side to side. This will cure the problem. A wipe with a cloth dipped in white spirits and then wrung out will clean off skirtings and other areas where the glaze has dripped. Make sure you clean any surface not supposed to be covered by the technique before the glaze hardens.

All the techniques described in this chapter are for use on walls that have first been prepared according to the instructions given in Chapter 1. The quantities given are for a room $3\,m \times 4\,m \times 2\frac{1}{2}\,m$ ceiling ($9\,ft \times 12\,ft \times 8\,ft$ ceiling). Quantities for other sizes of room are given on page 120.

STIPPLING

Of all the glazing effects practised today, stippling is still the one seen most often in the home. However, this does not mean it is the simplest or easiest effect to achieve. Of the many techniques described in this book, other than dragging, stippling is the most difficult to keep constant in both application and colour, although it is easier to control on furniture and small objects than on walls. For the beginner wanting to stipple a large surface area, the assistance of a friend or partner to brush on the glaze is a great help; one pair of hands brushing and roller blending, while the other does the stippling.

Remember that whatever tool is employed to redistribute the glaze, you are also taking colour off the wall, and to be absolutely successful in doing this, your own skill and artistry will play a major role.

Stippling.

800 ml (1½ pt) white spirits
6 tablespoons scumble glaze
  (commercial variety)
3 tablespoons artists' oil paint (mixed
  separately in a little white spirits)
or
800 ml (1½ pt) home-made glazing
  liquid (see page 12)
3 tablespoons artists' oil paint (mixed
  separately in a little glazing liquid)

good quality 10–12 cm (4–6 in)
  paintbrush
sponge roller or similar
stippling brush
paper towels or rags
white spirits
bucket, bowl or polythene container
step-ladder

When stippling, the transparency of the pigment and glaze should give a flattening soft bloom to a flat or opaque surface. This subtle quality looks its best when tints and shades of the colour used for the glaze stay within the same colour family as the base coat already on the wall. Mistakes made when using contrasting colours, no matter how small, tend to stand out at first glance.

Mix the glaze and oil colour the night before you want to use them (see pages 12–13).

One person applies the glaze, starting at ceiling level and working downwards and outwards. A strip 1 m (3 ft) wide is enough for the beginner to tackle. (In cold conditions or humid weather, larger areas can be covered.)

Roller this area to take away the stripes left by the brush. (The surface will now look stippled, but unless you are adept at using a roller there is always the fear that a slip line will spoil the surface, plus the fact that in almost every room there are places a roller cannot get into.)

The person stippling now starts at the top of the wall, moving down and out with a light tapping motion, blending again the area of glaze that has been applied.

While the stippler works this strip, the assistant starts to brush and roller the next strip, working from the skirting upwards and outwards. This ensures you are not getting in each other's way and only using one pair of steps instead of two. The secret of success is to make sure at all times that the edge of the glaze you have just applied is kept wet, enabling you to blend it easily with the adjacent strip.

Work in this way until the room is completely stippled.

Check for drips and spills; clean off where necessary.

Allow the surface to dry, then seal with an appropriate varnish (see page 121).

DRAGGING

Fine graduated lines pulled down the length of a wall, using a large long-haired brush, is the total statement expected of dragging. Done well, it can considerably change the dimensions of a room. Ceilings lift skywards; panelling becomes luxuriously monumental.

To say that this technique takes many hours of practice is no overstatement. A steady hand and a good eye are needed before attempting anything on a grand scale. The correct brushes make a difference of course, and these are very expensive for the novice. The preparation of the surface must take priority for dragging to be a total success, every crack, lump and bump will appear through the striped effect produced by this technique.

Mix the glaze the night before you want to use it, adding the colour a little at a time (see pages 12–13).

Do try a test piece before you start in order to get the colour exactly right. 'Near enough' might be the downfall of what could have been a wonderfully coloured room.

One person applies the glaze, starting at ceiling level and working downwards and outwards, in a strip approximately 1 m (3 ft) wide.

Roller this area from top to bottom, blending in any unevenness in the application of the glaze colour.

Dip the flogger into the glaze to the depth of 1 cm (½ in); gently wipe off the glaze leaving the tips of the flogger moist and slightly splayed. This prevents you lifting off too much of the glaze on the first strip.

Keeping the pressure the same at all times, draw the flogger as straight and as steadily as you can, down the wall. If you cannot

The subtleties of an olive green glaze over an apricot base coat give a gentle quality to a town house sitting-room.

800 ml (1½ pt) white spirits
6 tablespoons scumble glaze
3 tablespoons artists' oil paint (mixed separately in a little white spirits)
or
800 ml (1½ pt) home-made glazing liquid (see page 12)
3 tablespoons artists' oil paint (mixed separately in a little glazing liquid)

good quality 10–12 cm (4–6 in) paintbrush
sponge roller or similar
flogger (brush) 6–12 cm (3–6 in) wide
paper towels or rags
white spirits
bucket, bowl or polythene container
step-ladder

manage this action all in one movement it sometimes helps if the brush can be taken by your assistant at floor level, who should then draw the flogger upwards through the glaze from the bottom. This has its problems, as you both need to maintain the same pressure, but it can work with practise.

Work in this way around the room until all the wall area is covered.

Check for runs, drips or spills, and clean off where necessary. Allow the surface to dry; then seal with an appropriate varnish.

Tips

Pin a plumbline from ceiling to skirting approximately 12 cm (6 in) away from the wet edge of the strip you are working on. This helps to keep your line straight at all times.

A wallpaper-hanger's smoothing brush can be used as a substitute for a flogger. And at one-fifth of the price, it is recommended for the person who is home decorating on a small scale.

If glaze has built up at the top and bottom of the wall and you find yourself with a narrow band of a different colour depth, you could fix a flat braid or webbing 2–3 cm (1–1½ in) wide, using spray adhesive (see pages 124–25), in a tone to suit the glaze or perhaps a contrasting colour picked out from the room's furnishings. This will certainly enhance an elegant room.

When small areas around doors and windows are being tackled, an ordinary 5 cm (2 in) paintbrush comes in handy. Using it dry, pull it through the glaze in the same way as the flogger.

RAGGING AND RAG-ROLLING

Ragging is by far the easiest technique for anyone learning to glaze and gives sensational results very quickly. The glaze is lifted off the wall with a soft cloth, leaving behind a dappled or facetted surface with great depth and personality. The fast application enables large areas to be covered with ease. It is a perfect solution for those landings and stairwells that can give problems with other techniques.

The best cloths to use are: interlock jersey (old T-shirts, vests, and so on are ideal), which gives a soft edge and an appearance of parchment; cottons and cheesecloth, which stay crisp in the fold, and vary in the effects they produce from soft islands with hard edges to

Ragging.

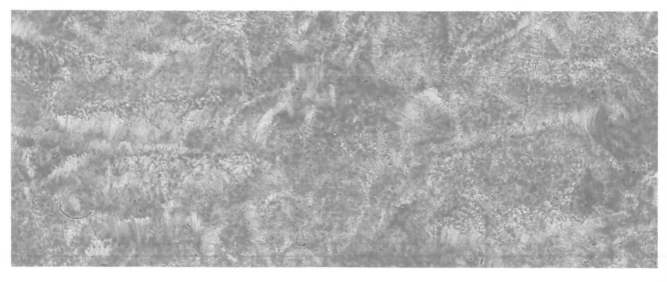

bold, hard lines resembling crazed stone. It is advisable to experiment with different cloths. This will give you hours of fun and enable you to find the cloth best suited to both you and the room.

A small room should not be too difficult to manage by yourself, although as always when glazing, an assistant or helper comes in handy for the areas that take time, like the backs of shelves and the fiddly corners around a door.

Ragging is done by bunching up a cloth or rag into your hand, then gently patting the surface glaze until an even dappling is achieved. When rag-rolling, the cloth is first of all wrapped into a sausage of folds, stitched or tied at either end, and rolled up and down the wall, lifting lines of glaze off the surface.

Mix the glaze and artists' oil colour together the night before you want to use them (see pages 12–13).

One person applies the glaze to the wall, starting at the ceiling and working downwards and outwards. A strip 1 m (3 ft) wide from ceiling to floor is enough to undertake at any one time.

Roller this strip over, blending in brush marks; give the edge that you will be working against an extra rolling over, which will help when blending the next strip.

Rinse and wring out your cloth. Starting at the top and patting gently, work down the wet glaze, regularly blotting the cloth on a paper towel or cleaning rags. Take care that you do not overwork an area as this will produce quite a lot of difference in the overall colour markings.

Brush on the next strip of glaze, blending over the previously applied and still wet edge. Roller out any colour build-up where these two edges meet. Carry on in this way until the whole room is covered.

Check for drips, runs or spills.

Wait for the surface to dry, then seal with an appropriate varnish (see page 121).

Tips

Do keep blotting the rag on a piece of kitchen roll; if it becomes really saturated, wring it out. If this is not done regularly the colour on the wall will be very uneven.

800 ml (1½ pt) white spirits
6 tablespoons scumble glaze
3 tablespoons artists' oil colour (mixed separately in a little white spirits)
or
800 ml (1½ pt) home-made glazing liquid (see page 12)
3 tablespoons artists' oil colour paint (mixed separately in a little glazing liquid)

good quality 10–12 cm (4–6 in) paintbrush
sponge roller or similar
rags of cotton jersey or similar
paper towels
white spirits
bucket, bowl or polythene container
step-ladder

Rag-rolling.

A sunny start to a day can always be had when the walls of a room are painted mellow yellow. A soft jersey cloth was used to create a dappled background that succeeds brilliantly in setting off furniture, fabrics and objects. To achieve this golden tone, a mixture of Naples yellow and Cadmium yellow (middle) were used over a base coat of buttermilk eggshell paint.

Rag-rolling

For this variation you use exactly the same method as for ordinary ragging until you start to remove the glaze from the wall. Then, with a hand at each end of the rolled-up cloth, and using the same movements as if you were rolling out pastry, you roll over the surface of the wet glaze. Moving backwards and forwards, avoid going over one area too much as this will bring more glaze off than necessary, creating a patchy effect.

Keep standing back from the work as you are covering the wall surface. Any dark patches can be dabbed over lightly to redistribute the glaze.

BAGGING

A novel twist to the more traditional ragging, bagging gives a surface of greater depth and textural effect. It is one of the simplest of all the glazing techniques. For walls in the alpine category (more lumps and bumps than wall), this glaze technique is a winner. Good preparatory work still applies, as the surface should be as smooth as possible, but discrepancies in the basic surface show less than with any other method of glaze application.

Brown paper bags, dipped in white spirits and wrinkled with the

Bold and sumptuous, the large range of tones achieved with one colour are indicated here with the use of a deep crimson glaze and a heavy-duty polythene bag. The base colour of the wall in this instance was off-white, which creates quite a dramatic look. Experiments with this method of glaze application will be really enjoyable.

800 ml (1½ pts) white spirits
6 tablespoons scumble glaze
3 tablespoons artists' oil colour
   (mixed separately with a little white
   spirits)
or
800 ml (1½ pts) home-made glazing
   liquid (see page 12).
3 tablespoons artists' oil colour
   (mixed separately in a little of the
   glazing liquid)

good quality 10–12 cm (4–6 in)
   paintbrush
sponge roller or similar
bag of choice
   – use the same bag for a whole job
   – if you are using polythene bags
   that have a name printed on the
   front, turn them inside out before
   use as the print may come off on
   the wall
paper towels or rags
white spirits
bucket or polythene containers for
   glaze
step-ladder

hands until soft give a close, cracked eggshell pattern; crumpled freezer bags give an effect similar to the crazing of a broken windscreen. High density polythene bags (supermarket and department store carrier-bags), create patterns ranging from crushed velvet to crazy paving. Colour combinations can be quite wild, with emphasis put on the dramatic: claret over a deep ochre, navy blue over emerald green. There is no end to the variations that can look outstanding and original with this technique.

Care must be taken on a large surface area. Blot the bag often, as you do not want to put colour back on the wall that has already been taken off.

Mix the glaze and oil colour together the night before you want to use them (see pages 12–13).

Apply the glaze to the wall with a brush, starting at the top and working downwards and outwards. An area 1–2 m (3–6 ft) wide can be covered at one time with this technique as it is done quickly. Large areas are covered within minutes once the glaze has been applied.

Roller over the wet glaze to blend in the colour, giving an even cover to the whole glazed surface.

If you start bagging at the top and work down the glaze may look lighter at ceiling height. It is better to start in the middle of the strip

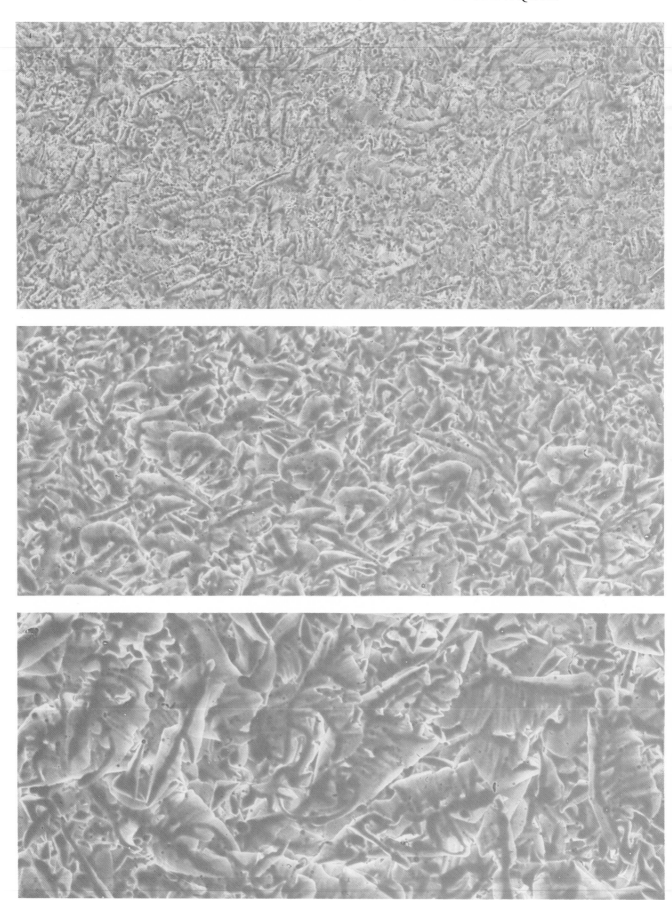

and pounce the bag over the surface working all over in circular movements. The bag can be turned in the hand to prevent the pattern becoming obviously symmetrical; or the hand can be turned on each pounce giving the same random patterning.

Stand back at intervals to make sure the colour is not too dense in some areas and not dense enough in others. Blot and pounce to give the glaze a constant coloured surface.

When completed, wait for the surface to dry and then seal with an appropriate varnish (see page 121).

Tips
Make a board 30 cm (12 in) square with handle on the back. Staple heavy-duty polythene sheeting to it and use this. It keeps hands clean and will cover the wall area even faster.

SPONGING

Out of the bathroom and onto the wall, the natural sea-sponge is an ideal tool for wall glazing. The distinctive speckled effect produced by the different-sized holes of a natural sponge can give a room casual elegance, compared to the classic formality of a stippled surface. A finish built up with two or more coats of sponged glaze gives a parchment or antique leather look. Carried to the extreme it may even resemble crumbling stone walls. Easy to achieve, quick to execute, sponging looks good in any room of the house.

If the beginner does not want to go to the expense of buying a large sea-sponge, a cellulose sponge split in half, like a sandwich cake, will do the job. And if you use both halves at the same time, one in each hand, the work will be finished quicker, and the glaze will not look too regimental. The soft, open-holed sponge is the one to use, as the closed-hole foam sponges do not give as free a translation of this technique.

Opposite:
Top: Bagging with a paper bag.
Centre: Bagging with a freezer bag.
Bottom: Bagging with a high-density polythene bag.

800 ml (1½ pts) white spirits
6 tablespoons scumble glaze
3 tablespoons artists' oil colour (mixed separately in a little white spirits)
or
800 ml (1½ pts) home-made glazing liquid (see page 12)
3 tablespoons artists' oil colour (mixed separately in a little glazing liquid)

good quality 10–12 cm (4–6 in) paintbrush
sponge roller or similar
natural sea-sponge, or large-holed cellulose sponge split in half
paper towels or rags for cleaning and blotting
bucket or polythene container
step-ladder

Sponging, applied in four layers over four consecutive days, make this room extra special. The first glaze used was yellow, followed by tangerine, then light red, and finally crimson.

The total look of sponging in a London dining-room. Undulating layers of colour worked from light to dark over an off-white base. Although to many four days may seem too time-consuming, the effect of this application of glaze is like no other wall covering.

Mix the glaze with the oil paint the night before you want to use them (see pages 12–13).

Starting at the ceiling, cover an area approximately 1 m (3 ft) wide. Brush the glaze onto the wall working down towards the skirting-board.

Roller this over, blending the glaze towards the outside to make it somewhat finer. This helps when it comes to applying the next strip of glaze.

Wet the sponge in water and squeeze it out. This prevents the

Opposite Combing.

sponge from absorbing too much of the oil glaze into the centre, which would make it very sticky, and in time flat and useless.

With light to medium pressure, pat the sponge against the wall surface. Take care that glaze does not build up on the sponge. Make sure you blot or wipe off any residue regularly.

Work in this way around the room, standing back occasionally to see if there are any discrepancies in the overall colouring of the glaze. Pat lightly to re-distribute the glaze if necessary.

Varnish when dry (see page 121).

Tips

For a room to fire the imagination of all who see it, try sponging the glaze in three or four different colours, one layer over another. Each coat should be allowed to dry and varnished over before the next is applied. A fabulous depth can be gained from this if using a high-sheen varnish; walls take on depth and a lacquered look.

COMBING

Records show ivory, wood and leather combs being used for decorative paintwork since ancient Egyptian times. For the beginner, nothing more than a piece of stiff cardboard and a pair of sharp scissors are needed. These simple tools will give you a patchwork quilt of pattern if you so choose.

A comb is made by cutting teeth of equal or unequal proportions along a straight edge of cardboard. Once cut, the cardboard comb can be worked through a surface glaze leaving the spaces between the teeth as colour on the wall. Wood graining is achieved by a similar process, although the tools and the methods used are considerably more complicated.

To experiment with this technique is the best way to learn about the glaze as a medium. Hours of enjoyment can be had, playing with different sized combs, crazy colour combinations, and varying patterns. Some specialist paint shops sell metal and rubber combs. If you are not pleased with the cardboard combs of your own making, try one of these.

800 ml (1½ pts) white spirits
6 tablespoons scumble glaze
3 tablespoons artists' oil colour
(mixed separately in a little white spirits)
or
800 ml (1½ pts) home-made glazing liquid (see page 12)
3 tablespoons artists' oil colour
(mixed separately in a little glazing liquid)

good quality 10–12 cm (4–6 in) paintbrush
sponge roller or similar
comb or combs of choice
paper towels or rags for cleaning
bucket or polythene container
step-ladder

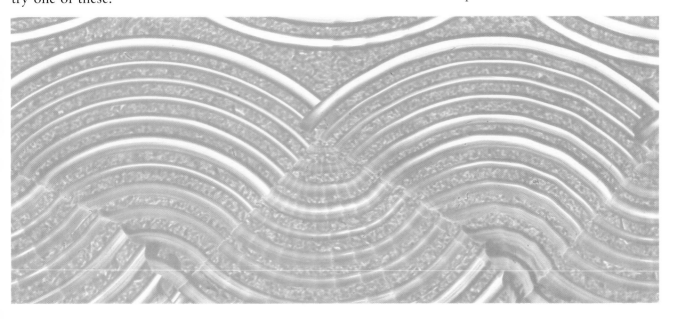

Mix the glaze and the oil colour the night before you want to use them (see pages 12–13).

Starting at the top of the wall and covering an area approximately 1 m (3 ft) wide, apply the glaze working down towards the skirting-boards.

Roller over the surface of the glaze to blend the brush strokes.

Comb the glaze in the design of your choice.

Clean up any spills or runs.

When the surface is dry, seal with a varnish (see page 121).

VARIATIONS ON A GLAZING THEME
(Different strokes for different folks)

There is no end to the range of effects that can be achieved by lifting an oil glaze off a surface. Using the same materials, glaze, brush and roller, the three methods known as basket weave, herring-bone and scallop-shell differ only in the individual brush strokes.

Apply colour glaze coat with a brush across the top of the wall, working a band 1 m (3 ft) deep at a time.

Roller over this horizontal band, blending the glaze as you go.

1.1 *Alternate vertical and horizontal brush-strokes give a basket-weave finish.*

1.2 *Diagonal criss-cross brushing produces a look of herring-bone parquet.*

1.3 *With the brush used like a compass, semi-circular scallop shapes appear.*

With a 6 or 10 cm (3 or 4 in) paintbrush stroke the glaze as shown in fig. 1.1, 1.2 or 1.3.

Cover one wall at a time, working in horizontal strips, from top to bottom.

Wait until dry, then seal with a varnish (see page 121).

Tips

Try these effects using a comb in place of a brush.

Basket-weave in two or three colours, applied one on top of the other, can look like tweed fabric: well worth experimenting with.

CLOUDING

Usually reserved for ceilings, this oil-based technique gives the effect of a cloudy sky, although it can look sensational in fantasy colours covering a whole room. A different approach is used for this glaze technique, quite similar in method to the background work for marbling (see page 72). The light, airy quality of clouds begin to lift a room from the earthly into the ethereal, developing a theme of tranquility and space.

One, two or three colours can be used if you become really adept. However, to keep things simple, start by using only one colour and perhaps tints or shades of that one colour. You will be amazed just how many tones can be achieved with a single pot of glaze.

Mix the glaze with the oil colour of your choice the night before you want to use them (see pages 12–13). If you are using different colours, keep them in separate jars or containers and remember to use one brush per glaze. This is most important as colours can easily start to look grey and muddy when the same brush is used for all the different colours.

Working in diagonal lines of varying width, brush on the glaze with uneven strokes (fig. 2.1). Leave at least 25 per cent of the base coat uncovered.

Complete the whole of one wall in this way.

When the glaze has reached a semi-dry state (tacky to the touch), take a soft cloth and blend it with a circular rubbing movement in the same way that a window-cleaner works with a chamois leather,

800 ml (1½ pts) glazing liquid or scumble and white spirits (see recipe on page 12)
10–12 cm (4–6 in) paintbrush
soft cloth (interlock jersey or similar non-woolly fabric)
white spirits
paper towels or rags

2.1 *Loose, uneven brush-strokes that vary in depth of colour is the first step.*

2.3 *To keep the feeling of floating clouds, work over a large area, viewing it occasionally from a distance.*

2.2 *A soft cloth rubbed over the semi-dry glaze creates the impression of light and space.*

Opposite: *Your feet can be well and truly on the ground but when you awake to find your head surrounded by clouds you may feel lightness in your step for the rest of the day. Aquamarine and cobalt blue mixed with white were the two glazes applied to the walls, ceiling and window-shutters in this bedroom. The base colour used is a very pale green, which adds interest to the light passages of the clouding, and gives scope for the introduction of a true white if a real cloud-like representation is called for.*

gently rubbing one area into another. In places a darker edge of glaze can be left, as in reality, with the sun behind them, clouds appear to have a distinctive, hard edge (fig 2.2).

The larger the area rubbed and blended in this way, and the quicker one band of glaze is worked into the next, the more likely you are to achieve the effect of life and vitality so reminiscent of a moving, cloudy sky.

Stand back at regular intervals to look at the flow and movement of the clouds. Do not worry if it appears slightly disjointed at first. The beauty of this glaze application is in the fact that it can be adjusted up to three or four hours after you first applied the glaze. If you decide that you have removed too much glaze in any one area, it is possible to give a quick brush over with more glaze and blend over it again.

Check over the walls for any drip or spills (there should not be any if you have used the cloth correctly), but do make sure whenever you finish a wall that all the glaze has been removed from areas of paintwork not decorated with the clouded effect.

Wait for the walls to dry; then seal with an appropriate varnish (see page 121).

Do not give up on this technique, it is the basis for many other interesting effects. And who knows, it may be the closest we will ever get to heaven.

PROBLEMS WITH OIL GLAZES

For those of you who are discovering that things are a little more difficult than you imagined, some problems and their causes are listed here. Check them over before becoming disheartened. The solution may prove to be quite simple and straightforward.

Glaze drying too fast

Temperature of the room is too high.
Too much white spirits in the glaze.
Too much drier has been used in the glaze (home-made recipe).
The glaze has been applied too thin.
Oil colour pigment is of the quick-drying kind.

Glaze drying slowly

Temperature of the room is too low; humidity in the room too great.
Excess linseed oil, scumble, or oil colour.
Glaze has been applied too thick.

Dark patches

Penetration of glaze due to surface being porous.
Artists' oil colour has not been mixed well enough before being added to the glaze.
Failure to wipe down cloth or roller in between working large areas of glaze.

Glaze running, or not staying fast on the wall

Too much white spirit.
Not enough scumble glaze (commercial variety).
Not enough whiting or linseed oil (home-made recipe).
Too much glaze applied.

Points to watch out for:

A skin may form over glaze that has been left to stand always strain through muslin or an old stocking before use.
Any dust or brush hairs should be left on the surface of the glaze until it is perfectly dry. They can be easily removed by wiping over the area with the flat of your hand. Use of a cloth, unless of fine quality, could leave fibres on the surface.

TIPS FOR SAVING TIME

There are tricks of the trade in most professions, and shortcuts made by many a craftsman may not always work for other individuals. These time-savers are based on the safest and most adaptable methods. You will probably find lots more once you start to work with glazes.

Use masking tape on skirting boards, around light switches, mouldings and cupboard or wardrobe fixtures in the room. This gives a neat edge and can save you a lot of time when you are cleaning up afterwards.

If carpets have been left down in the room and you want to stipple a skirting board, take a large sheet of mounting card and hold it at an angle between the carpet and skirting board while applying and working the glaze. This will stop the glaze running onto the carpet. It also prevents the brush and glaze from collecting carpet hair and dust as you work.

Clean up drips and spills as you go along, rather than leaving it until the whole room is finished. This way you do not miss any areas and the glaze does not have a chance to dry out.

Never work in a room with furniture left around the walls. Move

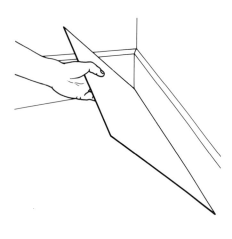

3 *Avoid glazing the carpet! A board placed between skirting and floor-covering will keep the colour on the surface it is intended for.*

everything into the middle of the floor space and cover with dust sheets before starting work.

If you do not finish the room in one day and you can continue on the next, leave your application brush in the glaze container overnight instead of cleaning it. This saves time and white spirits. Alternatively, put the brush into a jar of clean water. Oil and water do not mix, therefore air will prevent the brush from drying out but will not penetrate the oil. A roller can be stored overnight by wrapping it in a length of paper towel soaked in white spirits and then in a polythene bag.

TIPS FOR SAVING MONEY

As an alternative to the costly bristle stippling brush, a rubber stippler is available at one-fifth of the price. Although a different surface effect is produced (more open in spacing between points), it still looks very attractive. For small areas, a splayed nylon-bristled paste brush gives a sufficiently good finish.

The flogger (brush used for dragging) is a pricy item. Unless you plan a career as a decorative painter, try an ordinary 12 cm (6 in) paintbrush or a wallpaper-hanger's smoothing brush (the longer the bristles, the better).

Do not throw away your cleaning spirits. As long as you have used it for glaze brushes only, save it and make it the base of your next glaze. The colour sinks to the bottom of the container in most cases, ready for you to decant if you wish. If you are wanting to mix a colour similar to the glaze you have used, then leave it as it is, and add the other ingredients until you have the quantity required for your next job.

Save all your left-over glazes for at least three months in case of accident in the room you have glazed. Never throw them away. Keep a melting pot and add any left-overs. The soupy shades can look great for that mellow, restful sitting-room or study. Remember to strain a glaze mixture if it has been stored for a while.

Containers: Empty polythene ice cream cartons, jam jars, coffee jars, aluminium trays from take-away food shops, washed out: all these come into service for mixing and storing decorative paint. Yoghurt and margarine containers should be avoided as the spirit content melts the plastic.

Save old clothes to use as cleaning rags. Sheets and shirts can be used to produce effects on a wall surface, or to cover furniture while you are working in a room.

3 WATER-BASED GLAZE TECHNIQUES

From Pompei to Portsmouth, stately home to humble dwelling, water-based paints have been used throughout the centuries to provide colour and decoration. Before the advent of the paints we know today (emulsions, vinyls and acrylics), pigments were being ground and mixed with water into paste and employed as a vehicle to cover all kinds of surface. The tempera paints (egg mixed with pigment) of altar pieces and frescoes were applied to gesso and wet plaster. Traces of amazingly bright, coloured paint has been found on the marble statuary of ancient Greece and Rome. In Chester Cathedral, there is a painting on a mesh of fine cobwebs. There is no end to the ways in which paint can be applied, or to the surface materials that can be covered. In this chapter the basic modern paints used are readily available and inexpensive. With a little imagination, they can transform a room from the dowdy into the sumptuous.

BASIC PREPARATION

Water-based paint sinks into any porous surface almost immediately. The fast drying-time enables a sizeable room to be completed within a couple of days. The instructions for use are stipulated by the different manufacturers on the paint containers. Needless to say, the elbow work and energy that are required before putting brush to wall can take longer than the painting itself. (You are only as good an artist as your canvas surface permits you to be.) The cracks and holes will have to be made good, and the surface rendered clean and dry.

New plaster
1   As new plaster has a very porous surface, thin down the first coat of paint with water (anything from 10 to 30 per cent, depending on manufacturer's instructions). Allow to dry.
2   Apply a second coat of water-based paint. Allow to dry (two to four hours).
3   Apply a third coat (unless sponging or ragging, in which case this coat may be omitted).

Plaster covered in water-based paint (made good, clean and dry)
1   Apply one coat of water-based paint thinned down with 10 per cent water. Allow to dry (two to four hours).
2   Apply a second coat.

Old plaster with a top surface of oil-based paint (made good, clean, dry and sanded down thoroughly)
1   Apply one coat of water-based paint thinned down with 10 per cent water, and with one teaspoon of washing-up liquid added for every 500 ml (1 pt) to stop the paint separating on the wall surface.

Allow to dry.
2 Apply a second coat without thinning.
3 If you are covering up a dark colour, a third coat may be needed. If a transparent water glaze is to be used, apply a third coat.

New lining paper (surface must be dry and dust free)
1 Apply one coat of water-based paint, thinned to manufacturer's specification. Allow to dry.
2 Apply a second coat of water-based paint. Leave to dry (two to four hours).
3 Apply a third coat.

NOTES ON USING WATER-BASED GLAZES

Keep a set of brushes and rollers for use with water-based paints only. This will help to keep them in good condition.

If you are mixing your own colours, artists' gouache paint is better than poster or powder paint mixed with water and added to a white base. Be careful not to exceed the quantity of water specified for the basic mix as this could cause problems.

The quantities given in this chapter are for a room 3 m × 4 m × 2½ m ceiling (9 ft × 12 ft × 8 ft ceiling).

STIPPLING

An old paintbrush, the bristles cut down to within 2 cm (1 in) of the metal band, is a useful tool when water-stippling. A thin mix of paint is picked up on the brush, wiped over a cloth, then pounced onto the wall. It can take some time to cover a large area with this method, but unlike an oil glaze the colour discrepancy caused by patches of paint build-up does not show, even when the paint is drying out.

Soft, muted colours and pastels can look charming, especially if you can manage two or three different tints applied on to the wall at the same time. The finished look is like a bird's egg speckle. It has a soft opaque quality, flattering to the defined edges of picture frames and furniture.

Stippling.

300 ml (12 fl oz) emulsion glaze (see pages 124–25)
300 ml (12 fl oz) water
1 litre (2 pt) water-based paint (colour of choice)
bucket or plastic container
cloth
brush for stippling (experiment until you find the one you prefer)

Empty the emulsion glaze and water into a plastic bucket or container and stir thoroughly. Add this to your chosen colour, or to individual tints in proportion to the number you are using. The mixture should resemble single cream in consistency. If it is too thick, add more water.

Dip the brush into the paint, and then wipe on a cloth to take off any excess. Too much paint on the brush will make it difficult to keep an even cover. If using a small brush, the maximum area you should attempt is 30 cm (12 in) square. A larger brush can cover a greater area. (If you make sample sheets before you start, you will be able to find out the approximate area covered per brush-load.)

Pounce the brush lightly over the surface until your brush starts to get dry. The effect to aim for is a soft speckling.

Keep repeating these same movements, re-loading the brush, wiping off and pouncing on, until you have covered the whole wall.

Stand back and make sure you have an even covering of colour.

With a cleaning cloth dipped in water, wipe over any flecks of paint that may have fallen on the skirting or other woodwork.

Wait until completely dry. The emulsion glaze used in this recipe acts as a sealer for the surface. This enables you, when cleaning, to wipe the walls down with a damp cloth.

SPONGING

This is a technique for anyone in the family to attempt. Sponging with water paint is great fun; messy on the hands, maybe, but easy on the eye when it is used for covering a wall. This technique was used quite widely after World War II when wallpaper was almost non-existent and very expensive. It is not as dramatic as ragging in appearance, but is certainly noticeable when entering a room.

Sea sponges are used as in oil glazing, although the size of the sponge in this instance is as important as the texture. A small sponge used as a blotter can leave its mark as a statement, in which case the wall becomes blotched at random with each colour or tint worked over or against one another. A large sponge is best suited to one colour only, applied over a base coat.

If you are working with more than one colour, you can apply them at different times through the day, using the same sponge and washing it out between colours. If doing this, it is easiest to work from the darkest colour to the lightest, and flaws in the consistency of application will not show.

300 ml (12 fl oz) emulsion glaze (see pages 124–25)
300 ml (12 fl oz) water
1 litre of water-based paint
bucket or plastic container
sponge or sponges
cloth for cleaning up
rubber gloves (optional)

Mix emulsion glaze with water and stir.

Add glaze and water to paint (colour(s) of your choosing).

Stir again thoroughly to make a consistency resembling single cream.

Take sponge and rinse first in water. Squeeze out and dip into mixture.

Apply to wall in patting movements. Try a large area, leaving spaces in between sponge, this will add to the effect if you are using more than one colour.

When you are using two or more colours, apply one colour first all the way around the room, then wash out sponge. Let the first colour dry (two to four hours), then proceed with the next colour.

Standing back, make sure the whole wall surface is evenly covered and that no large patches of plain colour show. It is not too difficult to blend over as long as you have mixed enough of each colour glaze to correct these mistakes.

RAGGING

To ring the changes on the decor of a room can be a costly affair. However, it does not necessarily have to be so if you use this quick and easy method. The colour you have grown tired of can soon be spruced up by simply ragging over with a fresh coat of paint.

Stir all recipe ingredients together in a container until thoroughly mixed.

Taking the cloth of your choice (experiment until you have found the one you feel happiest with), gently pat the glaze onto the surface of the wall, leaving as much colour definition as you can between the base coat and the glaze.

Try to complete a good large area at a time without letting the cloth dry out. If the wall was painted several years earlier it will soak up the glaze on contact with the cloth. On the other hand, if the surface does not hold the glaze, a possible build-up of oil or grease could be the reason. Add a drop of washing-up liquid to the glaze that you are applying.

Work the patting movements all over the wall, changing the position of the cloth in your hand in order to keep the effect as random as possible.

Keep standing back to make sure the effect is evenly distributed and clean up the spills and drips as you go along. With all the water-based techniques you do lean towards the messy.

Very interesting effects can be produced by utilizing fabric that already has a heavily textured surface. Any cloth is suitable as long as it does not have loose fibres or a woolly surface. Macramé lace, nylon curtain lace and some old sculptured velvets are past examples of people's ingenuity when employing this water-paint method.

300 ml (12 fl oz) emulsion glaze (see pages 124–25)
300 ml (12 fl oz) water
1 litre (2 pt) water-based paint, colour of your choice
bucket or plastic container
cloth for ragging
kitchen roll or rags for cleaning
step-ladder

Ragging.

SPECIAL EFFECTS WITH WATER-BASED PAINT

Textured paint is being employed frequently in new buildings. Rollers have been modified to cater for these speciality paints, giving a ridged or rippled surface. To many the idea of using a decorative effect over the top of these would seem odd, but, in the right setting, they can offset a piece of antique furniture or a painting in a way no other type of paint can. The following are not true glazes, but in many ways they are just as transparent.

On a granular surface paint
Apply one coat of water-based paint (thinned). Allow to dry.

Take a coloured wax candle or a wax crayon and rub it over the surface. Shiny wax over a matt paint glows with a strange light and gives even greater depth and texture.

On a ridged and rippled surface
Apply one coat of thinned, water-based paint.

Using tinted furniture wax of the type used to give antique finish (see list of suppliers, page 124–25), on a nail or shoe-polish brush, gently scrub over the surface in circular movements.

Buff with a clean, bristle brush to a silky sheen.

On plasterwork in high relief (already sealed)
It is difficult to work with a brush or crayon over this thickly textured covering but original effects can be obtained by using watercolour paint very thinly applied through a house-plant spray. A surface can be covered quickly, the colour building up in the natural recesses of the plaster. A chamois leather or sponge can be used to rub over the top surface, lifting off any excess paint.

4 STENCILLING

In today's sophisticated world, where mass production plays an ever-increasing role, the churning out of decorative art with little or no character seems to be taking precedence over imaginative design and good colour sense. Yet looking back in time, some of the humblest materials were used without any trace of sophistication, to give results that even today are a joy to look at. The freshness and child-like charm of early pattern-making has a purity seldom equalled by today's machinery.

Stencilling, along with potato and stick printing, wood and lino cuts, belongs to the home-base of traditional repeat patterning for decorative purposes. It is difficult to say when or where the first stencils were used, but the art of stencilling has been practised for many centuries. America, Japan and India have all created individual looks and techniques. The pioneers of America used primitive shapes and colours to execute their stencils. Furniture and walls were covered with designs ranging from simple geometric to primitive nature studies. In Japan, intricate webs of stylized delicacy were cut in oiled paper, many thicknesses at the same time, and used by dyers to pattern cloth for garments of great beauty. India, known for its spices and silks, produced stencils on a vast scale. Trees and birds with extravagant plumage lived gaily on curtains, bedcovers and ornamental garden tents. In England, the early Victorians, searching for a different set of values relating to the past, turned to the spiritual Middle Ages. With the aid of stencils and fine craftsmen, palaces, churches, and country houses were made to dazzle and delight under many a stencilled blanket.

In the 1980s, the vogue for stencilwork has infiltrated the family home once again, being inventive and original, and pulling away from the machine-made monotony of patterned wallpapers and the austere plains of the Scandinavian teak and hessian influence. Stencils are being treated to a new lease of life, covering walls or used as frieze and panel designs, in making personal patterned statements on fabrics and objects ranging from plant pots to yacht sails.

Books of stencil patterns are available (see page 124–25). These can be cut out and used instantly, as the pages are printed on oiled paper. Alternatively, you can design your own. It is not important to be able to draw expertly when stencilling. It is quite acceptable to trace a design or pattern from a magazine or book. The basic materials are simple and the method is easy enough to be practised by a five-year-old. For a small expenditure, a boundless world opens up.

MATERIALS

Stencilling card It is not difficult to find stencil paper. Most of the craft/artist supply shops carry the thickish oiled card in sheet form, approximately 60 × 90 cm (2 × 3 ft) in size. Do remember, when buying the card in this way, to keep it flat. Once rolled up, it is not easy to straighten out, and the card must lie flat against the wall when stencilling.

4.1

4.2

4.3

Stencil film Not so easy to find as card, this transparent film of thick celluloid, is available at many D-I-Y shops. It is more expensive than the card, but not prohibitively so if only a small area is to be stencilled.

The bonus of being able to see through it makes it easier to place the stencil when using more than one colour. For more complicated designs, success depends on the design being matched up correctly.

Stencil film with adhesive For problem areas such as convex or concave surfaces. Being adhesive on one side, it makes stencilling easy although it is not recommended for more than one application of colour. Cylindrical surfaces, candlesticks and storage jars are particularly suited to this way of stencilling. However, it is not cheap, and you do not get the same wear out of it as with the other materials.

Cardboard Thin glossy cardboard or card that has a metallic finish to it. It can be used for stencilling if treated with care. It should not be used for more than three or four applications of paint, but good results have been achieved on quite large areas. Alternatively, for the sake of economy when covering a large area, ordinary cartridge paper can be used. It is easy to cut with a scalpel or blade, and as long as you remember to keep the paint on the brush as dry as possible, your result should be very good.

Stencil brushes Most often seen are the small barrel-shaped brushes with thick hogs' hair bristles somewhat similar in appearance to a miniature shaving-brush although the hair is completely flat across the top. As an alternative, a 2 cm (1 in) wide household paintbrush with the bristles cut down to approximately 2 cm (1 in) can be used. The softer the bristle on the brush, the lighter the pouncing movement must be. If you bang down the bristle too heavily, your brush will become splayed and you will find it difficult to keep a clean edge.

For those who will be stencilling large areas bigger brushes with quite soft hair are available. These are expensive items to treat roughly, and the beginner would be best advised to try the small brush or the improvised household brush first.

PAINTS

Every type of paint can be used for stencil work. Through experience you will find the one you most prefer to work with. In some cases, the surface to be stencilled will be the deciding factor. This being so, a good rule to keep in mind is to put like materials together. On water-based surfaces such as emulsion paints, paper, and most fabrics (being porous), you would use a water-based stencil paint, poster paint, gouache, acrylics or emulsion. On oiled-based surfaces you would use gloss paint, artists' oil colours, enamel model paints, acrylics (undiluted) and spray car paints.

For fabric stencilling a number of craft suppliers stock special fabric printing dyes. These are used in the same way as paints. Wonderful effects can be produced using thinned acrylics on fabric, although a build up of acrylic paint makes the fabric lose its supple quality. For the experienced, waterproof drawing ink sprayed on with an aerosol canister can give sensational shadings and sharp outlines to the finest of silk chiffons.

Glass paints (see pages 124–25) can be used to stencil directly onto windows for a stained-glass look.

CHOOSING A DESIGN

A single, uncomplicated motif that can be repeated to make a border design, or placed at random on a wall as stars cover the sky, would be best to start with. It is advisable to keep to the simplest of shapes, ie, a leaf, a flower-head, geometrical triangles, diamonds, squares and circles. Before starting on a grand scale, experiment on paper until you have discovered how the brush and particular paint chosen, work for you. If you load your brush with too much paint half way through a border pattern, your chances of success will be ruined. In addition, many stencils look fine as stencils but lose decorative quality when seen on a wall in paintwork, and sample sheets can be a blessing in righting design faults that may not be obvious in the stencil itself.

In searching for designs, look closely at your everyday surroundings. There are hundreds of shapes and patterns that, without too much work, will create wonderful motifs. Sitting in your kitchen are spoons, teapots, bottles and, of course, a ready-made stencil in itself – the paper doylie. Children's books and comics are a treasure-chest of bold, inventive yet simple designs. For the more experienced, library research into books on the history of textiles, wallpapers,

Opposite One design, but two stencils, have been used in this country house kitchen. The bows and ribbons were stencilled first using blue acrylic paints; followed by the green floral motif, also in acrylic paint. The mid-sheen, oil-based paint was white, and sealed totally on completion of stencil work with two coats of Rowney Cryla matt varnish.

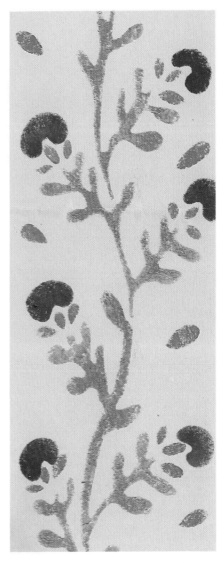

Far left For a design with more than one colour (see above)
4.1 *Stem and leaf motif traced onto stencil card and cut out.*
4.2 *Second-colour stencil of leaves around the flower head cut separately; matching-point notches are snipped from the sides of the stencil.*
4.3 *Third-colour stencil: traced, applied to stencil card, cut and notched.*

Simple geometric and straight-line stencils show how effective one colour used tonally can be.

Opposite: *Stencilled canvas impersonating a Kelim rug is an inexpensive way to cover a floor. Sealed with seven coats of polyurethane varnish, the canvas will take a great deal of wear and tear, including a wash-down every now and then.*

picture travelogues on the Far and Middle East are packed with a fantastic number of inspirational ideas. Unexpected but well worth looking at are the diagrammatic pages in mechanical engineering and biology reference books.

DRAWING OUT AND CUTTING A STENCIL

stencil card
tracing-paper
scalpel or sharp blade (xacto blade)
hard pencil (4H)
soft pencil (HB)
square of glass or cutting-pad
masking-tape
felt-tipped pen

Once you have chosen your design, clear an area large enough to lay down your square of glass or pad and to move the sheet of stencil card around in a circle without hitting anything. This is essential if you are trying to cut a design with curves in it. Work standing up if possible as the correct pressure for handling a cutting blade is easier to achieve.

Draw or trace the design lightly onto tracing-paper with the soft pencil. If you draw directly on to the card and make a mistake, it can become quite messy and difficult to rub out the discrepancy. Once you have your motif on the tracing-paper, line it with the soft pencil so that the line becomes well defined and quite a large amount of lead is left on the paper.

If you are using the transparent film for your stencil, put the film over your tracing-paper and use a felt-tipped pen to transfer the motif onto the film.

If you are using card, place the tracing-paper pencilled side down on the stencil card and hold in place with masking tape. Working with the hard pencil again, go over the motif with heavy pressure until all the lines have been drawn again. Lift off the tracing paper and you are left with the motif drawn in reverse on the card.

If using the film, you will have the design as your original drawing, not in reverse.

To cut the design out, place the card, film or paper on the glass or cutting pad. Take the blade or scalpel and hold it vertically over the card or film using only the very point of the blade itself. The reason for this is to make sure that the cut is clean and straight. If the blade edge is tilted from side to side when cutting there is every possibility that the paint will go underneath the stencil and make the edge rather woolly. If you are sitting down to cut stencils, this side movement tends to happen more often. When cutting a curved edge or a small spot, move the card or film around the blade rather than the blade around the card or film. It is very difficult to keep a continuous movement when cutting small circles. Some stencil-cutters have special circular punches for taking these very small areas out, but in the beginning it is better to keep to the very easy shapes and avoid the laborious and fiddly little shapes of more complex designs.

A mention must be made here of the stay-bars which are used to hold stencils together when dealing with large areas and circular motifs. If you have a design with large areas of stencil missing, it will develop weak spots once it has been used more than three or four times. This can create problems unless the stencil is strengthened in some way. The Japanese kept their fragile paper stencils firm by sandwiching strands of human hair in a fine mesh-like structure between two sheets of oiled stencil paper. If any area of the stencil might become fragile because of its greater size, try to incorporate attractive stay-bars into the design to strengthen the stencil (fig. 5). Do not think of the bars as a hindrance to your stencil; make use of them in a creative way.

If you have more than one colour in your design and have cut more than once stencil to accommodate this, make sure you notch in a matching point.

5.1 *To emphasize the form of the design, curved stay-bars strengthen the cut stencil and at the same time become an additional design element.*
5.2 *Without respect for stay-bar placing, straight cuts look severe and out of keeping with the spiral motif.*

1

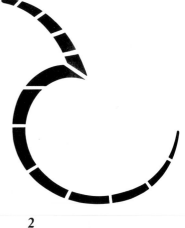

2

Once the cutting is complete, turn the stencil over and check to see if there are any woolly edges or areas that the blade has chamfered and tidy these up before using it. A sample sheet will help to identify them.

APPLYING PAINT

Once you have tried out your stencil on paper or card and are satisfied with the result, the hard work really starts. Place the stencil in position and secure it with a small amount of masking-tape so it cannot move. However, if you are stencilling onto ordinary wall-paper, do not use masking-tape as it could damage the surface on removal; use your free hand.

cut stencil
paint
soft cloth or paper towels
stencil brush
rags
masking-tape

Make sure all the materials you require are on hand and, if you happen to be up a ladder and have no room for your paints, make sure someone else is there to help you when the time comes to re-load your brush with paint.

The first important point to remember when applying paint for stencilling is that a little goes a long way. Never work with a brush that is packed with paint. A slow build-up of fine speckles is so much pleasanter to look at, and the gentle shading of fine layers of paint are the most attractive part of a stencil. Keep a cloth or paper towels by your side and for every brush-load of paint, dab the bristles on the cloth until the brush-head looks dry.

Pastel colours do not seem to register at all when you have the area covered with stencil card, but as soon as you lift the card off the area being stencilled, they can stand out quite strongly. Your sample sheets will help you judge just how far you can go with certain colour applications.

Pouncing is the term used to describe the movement of the stencil brush: firm but not too hard. The brush is tapped against the surface, working from the edges of the cut-out shape into the middle. With the soft, American style of brush, the movement used is more of a soft, circular, rolling movement, but this is generally used only on larger areas. If you have a floral theme in mind, or a design that should look three-dimensional, the brush strokes can be changed, working from the centre of a flower-head with your darkest application, to almost a mist-like transparency on the petal edges. Similarly, if the design is a bowl of fruit or flowers and you wish to give depth, then shade with one colour by working the brush over the same area two or three times.

The effect of stencil work can vary from a very flat surface with primitive child-like application, to shading with such subtle tones that an object starts to look real and alive.

When removing the stencil, take great care to lift it off vertically, otherwise you might smudge the edges of the design and spoil it. Wipe off any excess paint from the card with a clean cloth ready for the next application.

Once you are adept at the art of stencilling in one colour, the next step is to use two or three colours for the same motif. Use a separate brush for each colour and apply one colour at a time, gently shading and blending one into the other. Flowers and fruit look beautiful when treated in this way. A more complicated procedure is to use more than one stencil for the same motif, keeping the colours separate and working one over the top of another.

Above and opposite *One of the more difficult kinds of stencil work, shown here, is a mixture of techniques and mediums. The base colour of the wall was white; the paint was ordinary water-based emulsion. A grey emulsion thinned down to a water consistency was applied with a cloth at random to 60 per cent of the wall area. This was followed with lemon yellow waterproof drawing ink sprayed through a diffuser. When the ink was dry the stencil was placed on the wall and sprayed with cellulose car spray, with patches of black Indian ink once again applied at random. Last of all, lemon yellow and scarlet red acrylic paints were stippled through the stencil to illuminate some of the darker areas.*

Tracing paper is a must for this way of stencilling as the motif drawn has to be retraced for every colour used and its patternings matched up perfectly by notches (see fig. 4).

Spray paints

These cellulose-based paints, generally used for car repairs, are fun and easy to work with. The drying time is short which allows stencil movement from one area to the next within moments. Vertical surfaces are best to work on as the canisters should always remain upright. If they are tilted, the spray clogs and large spots of spluttered paint can mar the surface and design of a stencil. Care must be taken to mask off any of the surrounding area likely to be exposed to the minute specks of spray. It is amazing how far the particles fly, even though the spray is directed towards the stencil.

Spray-on cellulose paint is the ideal choice for metal surfaces such as kitchen trays and storage tins. Sealed with a clear cellulose or a polyurethane varnish, they can be wiped down with a damp cloth without damage to the stencilled work. To shade and use more than one colour with these paints is quite a challenge, as too much spray paint in one area can form nasty drips that can only be removed with special cellulose thinners, and in doing this the whole motif may have

to come off. Practice with these can improve your spraying perform-ance and enable you to achieve a professional look in a very short time.

IDEAS FOR WALLS

Borders around walls at ceiling height are the most commonly seen stencils, but taking the idea one step further, try stencilled panels around a room or around door-frames and skirting-boards (see pages 51–52). To ring the changes on those plain, bathroom wall-tiles, stencil your individual motif at random or all over the tiles. As long as they are sealed with two or three coats of varnish, they should be water-resistant. Stencils can re-vamp the dowdiest-looking tiles and give them a new lease of life.

STENCILLED WALL CLOTHS

Unprimed canvas or calico, or even old sheets, are suitable for stencil work with water-based paints, Acrylics come into their own here as they are for the most part washable. Wall cloths, being alternatives to the framed pictures and prints that hang in most homes, have their background in the tapestries of centuries ago. In the twentieth century, as works of decorative art, they add a soft edge to walls and windows, and can range from child-like humour to elegant hangings. Alternatively, the fabric can be attached to a base of thin polyester quilting and then thrown over furniture and beds in place of loose covers and quilts.

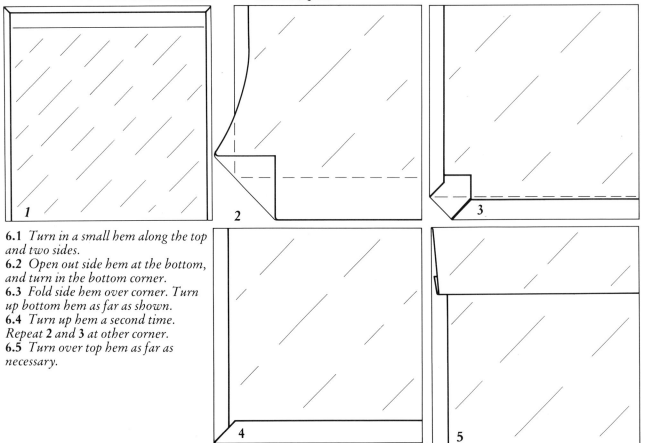

6.1 *Turn in a small hem along the top and two sides.*
6.2 *Open out side hem at the bottom, and turn in the bottom corner.*
6.3 *Fold side hem over corner. Turn up bottom hem as far as shown.*
6.4 *Turn up hem a second time. Repeat 2 and 3 at other corner.*
6.5 *Turn over top hem as far as necessary.*

canvas, calico or old sheets
cut stencil
paints or fabric dyes
brushes
needles
cotton

Take the fabric and turn a 5 cm (2 in) hem on all four sides. If you want a thick quilted or padded look, baste the material together with cotton or polyester wadding and fold the edges over, mitring the corners to make them less bulky. Leave a 6 cm (3 in) strip of fabric along the top edge. This will be turned over later, to take a pole, or rings if the wall-cloth is to hang from hooks.

Once you have drawn out your design, and cut the stencils, place them on the cloth and start colouring.

DOOR CLOTHS

These cloths can be used to simulate curtains and the traditional but rarer tapestries known as *portières* which were produced to cover the draughty gaps between door and frame, or to drape in place of doors between rooms.

First draw your stencil design, to fit the dimensions of windows or door, on tracing-paper. Once satisfied with the design, transfer it onto stencil card and cut it out. From this make a test piece of cloth, trying out your paint until you have the right consistency for the

canvas, calico or old sheets
cut stencil
paints or fabric dyes
brushes
needles
cotton

Acrylic paints used over an oil-based glaze applied to canvas are stencilled to duplicate the look of old tapestry. Hand-painted leaves and flower centres relieve the hard edges and give freedom to the overall design.

fabric. Then stencil directly onto your cloth. If your design is to surround a door or window, stencil one half and then reverse the stencil for the other half. In this case, make sure the stencil is dry and clean on the side you have already stencilled before laying it in reverse.

STENCIL WORK ON FABRIC

Fabric paints and screen-printers' dyes can be used to stencil fabrics as varied as velvet and the finest silk. Acrylic paint diluted with water or thinning agent can work equally well as long as the paint is mixed to the right consistency for the particular piece of fabric.

Cloths vary in absorbency and problems with paint colour may arise; for example, the paint may bleed into areas around the stencil. Always work on a sample of cloth first and test how the paint reacts to the fabric. Delicate effects can be produced with waterproof drawing inks sprayed on with a diffuser, giving a fine speckled finish. Subtle, mist-like blends of colour are the trade mark of this technique. Over-spraying in more than one colour can look sumptuous.

From your wardrobe and windows, the fabrics of discarded clothes or tired and faded curtains can be excitingly brought out of retirement and given new zest by stencilling.

Co-ordinate your bedroom by using a stencilled border on a bed valance, curtains and cushions, taking the motif from the wallpaper. Individuality of this kind is priceless, and the hours spent perfecting and pouncing give you a real sense of achievement.

Try a sample first to make sure your paint or dye is not going to run on the cloth.

Spread brown paper or newspaper on a flat surface. Pin the fabric down, or secure it with masking-tape, so that it cannot slide or move. Lay the stencil in place and tape at least two of the edges to hold it still while you are working.

If you are spraying, as in the waterproof drawing-ink technique, you may need to put small weights on parts of the stencil card to prevent it lifting. Remember that paint has a nasty habit of creeping under the edge of a stencil and this really ruins a design.

STENCILWORK ON WOOD AND METAL

Many a transformation from the ugly into the elegant and fashionable has taken place with the aid of paint and stencilwork, and amongst the different surfaces of wood and metal you will find a large selection of surfaces waiting for your imagination and nimble fingers.

The paint varies according to the surface, but if you keep to water-based paint for porous surfaces, and oiled-based paint for non-

flat working surface
cut stencil
screen-printers' ink, or acrylics mixed with thinning medium or water
fabric
paints
stencil brushes
cloth or paper towels
drawing pins or masking-tape
brown paper or newspaper

A child's desk painted off-white has had a fresh, delicate vine and flower motif applied. The curtains, blinds and bed valance in the room were the inspiration for the decorative border, and the acrylic colours were matched with these to carry the design onto the desk.

porous surfaces, you should eliminate any problems. Cellulose paints (spray canisters) are especially good on metal surfaces, but can be applied to almost everything. Acrylic paints can be used on both types of surface, but can peel if not suitably sealed when used on metal.

It is fun to brighten up objects around the home and it need not cost a fortune. Surface preparation is time-consuming, and is a task ill-suited to those who get bored quickly. There are some pieces of furniture and objects that need no preparation other than a wipe with a damp cloth or a light rub down with wire-wool before stencilling.
Wooden floors, furniture, and other wooden objects It is advisable to seal all new woodwork with a primer sealer if it is to be painted. If the wood will be seen as natural, a clear varnish sealer should be used either before you stencil, or afterwards to protect both wood and paint.

ROLLER-BLINDS

Fabric roller-blinds provide an ideal surface to stencil. Don't be afraid of displaying your creative style and imagination to the neighbourhood.

Proceed as with other stencilwork (see page 41).

acrylic paint
stencil brushes
waterproof drawing ink
diffuser
cut stencil
cloth for wiping stencil

Tips
Always work on a flat surface, and secure both blind and stencil in position while working.
Leave to dry for as long as possible before re-hanging the blind.
If you make a mistake, don't attempt to rub it off. Disguise it with paint mixed to the same colour as the blind, or add an extra motif to cover the area of the fault.

STENCIL WORK ON LEATHER

Leather has been decoratively painted for centuries, on walls, screens and clothes, and the soft, durable skin has been covered in every kind of design and device. And it is now as fashionable for furniture and garments as it ever was in the past. Many an imaginative paintwork display is provided by the back of a motorcyclist on his black leather jacket. In a simple way, surfaces nearer to home such as shoes, bags, book-covers and luggage, can be stencilled to relieve a plain surface.

Proceed as for other stencilwork.
Once the paint is dry and without moving the stencil if possible, seal the design with a polyurethane sealer on top of the paint but avoid contact with the rest of the leather surface. A wax furniture polish can help seal paintwork on leather, but a sample must be tested before attempting to apply this to the garment or object, in case the paint colour changes.

commercial shoe dyes, or acrylic
paints, or spray-on cellulose paint
stencil cut from self-adhesive stencil
film or card
brushes
cloth for cleaning stencil card if used

CERAMIC SURFACES (LAMP-BASES, TILES, VASES, PLANT-POT HOLDERS)

Unlike a porous surface, where paint immediately bonds with the object by being absorbed, ceramics are produced especially to repel moisture of any kind. Therefore they need not be sealed before being

stencilled, but they do need special treatment after stencilling.

Bearing in mind that like goes with like, do not try to work with water-based paints. Acrylic paint and cellulose are the mediums to use on this type of base coat.

Alternatively, you could use an oil-glaze base over the ceramic surface, and stencil in oil paint. A stippled oil glaze with a pattern stencilled over it can completely change the most mediocre tile and alter your bathroom beyond recognition within two or three days.

Mix the glaze according to the instructions in Chapter 1 (see page 12), and leave overnight to amalgamate.

Glaze the surface of the objects according to one of the techniques described in Chapter 2 (i.e., stippling, sponging, bagging). Allow at least twenty-four hours to dry.

Mix oil colours for the stencil work. Apply the stencil to surface, holding it in place with either masking-tape or your fingers. Load the brush and pounce the colour onto a cloth until the excess paint is removed, and then begin to stencil.

When the stencilling is complete, seal with Cryla matt or gloss varnish or polyurethane.

Oil paints take longer to dry than water-based paints, so allow some time before you varnish. Different pigments also have different drying times, so to be on the safe side, wait a week or so before varnishing.

oil-based paint
oil glaze
cut stencil and stencil brush
brushes or cloths to give background
    texture
masking-tape

Wall tiles that were in poor condition have been given two coats of eggshell paint followed by a soft cream glaze and worked on with artists oil colours to form an imaginative and different appeal to a bathroom wall. The sealer used over the whole surface was a polyurethane varnish applied three weeks after the original painting was completed.

5 SPECIAL EFFECTS

POOR MAN'S GOLD

Without looking too ostentatious, a little gold around the house helps create the illusion of luxury. The effect of light playing across a golden surface has dazzled every civilization and been worshipped as much as any sun, moon or star. However, gold leaf work is a specialist job requiring an apprenticeship of many years to achieve perfection. In addition, the tools and materials are very expensive.

As second best for the golden look, we have brass – the yellow metal of door knobs and knockers – which can be polished to a mirror finish. This metal is also available in a dust form known as 'bronze powder'. It is the base for a medium imitating gold, and has many uses. It can be bought in a range of colours and metal finishes, as well as in three shades of gold: pale, medium and dark.

The powder is fine, and a little goes a very long way. As stencil work requires the bronze powder in a liquid form, an additional medium must be used (most manufacturers do provide a suspension medium). This remains workable for quite some time and can be mixed with the powder to your own requirements, from the thinnest water-like consistency to a thick paste. Another fluid that can be mixed with bronze powder is 'emulsion glaze'. This PVA-based sealer is a perfect medium for poor man's gold as it does not give the flat, slightly tarnished effect to the pale gold.

Using it on a vast scale, you could turn a room into an Islamic mosque. On a small scale, you could paint a picture-frame, or stencil stylized flowers on a piece of velvet for an evening jacket or a cushion. The tooling of real gold on leather desks, books and tables can be simulated with stencil work. Many people find that the pleasure and enjoyment that this rich medium offers, brings out their most creative streak.

phial of bronze powder (also available in large quantities) (see pages 124–25)
small amount of emulsion glaze
stencil card if applicable
artists' brush or stencil brush
basin or saucer for mixing glaze and powder

Pages 51 and 52 Bronze powders in two shades, mixed with two different mediums, were used for this fantasy study based on four Islamic domes. The application of a rich red brown glaze in a herring-bone pattern radiating from the centre of the room also helped in the creation of a circular movement, turning the room into a dome. In all, 320 different stencils were used for the one room.
(cont'd on page 53)

There are no rules regarding quantities or consistency. A thin mix will give a fine covering and will be able to cover a large surface area. Small brushes can be used to give minute detailing. A thick paste-like mix will be best suited to stencilling and if really stiff when applied generously, will look like the modern textured gold of today's jewelry.

If painting free-hand, use artists' brushes and paint as normal, on all surfaces other than cloth.

When stencilling, the usual pouncing action is used; remember to clean excess paint off the brush with a cloth after loading. It becomes increasingly difficult to remove bronze powder when it has been suspended in emulsion glaze and the build-up on a stencil can severely distort a design. For this reason, keep a damp cloth or paper towels handy for wiping down the card or film as you use it.

When working on fabric, do not leave the fabric loose. Pin it down, or use masking-tape to keep the cloth as taut as possible. It is easier to stencil the design onto fabric than to paint by hand; the mixture for fabric should be medium/thick.

Alternative suggestions for the bronze powder enthusiast

For an extra-fine finish and a look of complete professionalism, try covering a non-porous surface with talcum powder, and then, with a paint-brush dipped into a Japan gold size, paint your design onto the object. Leave until the gold size is just on drying, then with a dry, soft-ended brush dipped into bronze powder alone, whisk lightly over the surface of the gold size, and leave to dry overnight. In the morning, take a slightly moist cloth and wipe away the talcum powder which has protected the surface from the spread of gold size, and you will be left with your poor's man gold so lightly applied to the surface it will look like gold leaf that has been rubbed off with age.

Mix bronze powder with black oil-based paint or stove enamel until you have the merest hint of a metallic glow. Paint over an entire surface with this and you will have the same effect as the most sought-after Japanese lacquer. To be really daring, try mixing bronze powder with white spirits and, while the paint is still very wet, load a brush with this, hold it 5–7 cm (2–3 in) above the surface, and tap it gently against a piece of wood to cover the surface evenly.

ANTIQUE LEATHER EFFECT AND PARCHMENT

During the sixteenth and seventeenth centuries, Cordoba leatherware was renowned throughout Europe. Dressed, pressed and painted to patterns of magnificent proportions, these leathers were much sought after for palace and grand house alike. Many museums show examples on furniture, although whole rooms had their walls resplendently hung with panels of leather, painted and gilded; lush fruits and flowers festooning joyously with parrots and monkeys. Alas, that age is past. The decorative leather industry is sadly depleted, and modern wallcoverings lack even the merest hint of their forebears.

Of course, not everyone wishes to have this riot of heavily-patterned leather on their walls, and the rather masculine appearance of this effect certainly changes the character of a room. In small amounts it can work to great advantage, transforming an old tin trunk or sea-chest into an Elizabethan court coffer. Used on a smaller scale still, a plywood cigar-box can take on the age-old patina and attraction of a Jacobean jewel box. Creating a quality that seems centuries old in two or three days, with the simplest of materials, is a real challenge and great fun can be had at the same time. Other advantages with this technique are the ease of cutting to fit odd shapes and corners, and the fact that areas as large as 3 × 1 metre (3 × 1 yd) can be produced without too much trouble (a large working surface is necessary for this size).

There are two methods of producing antique leather. You will probably have the necessary materials in the house already, with the exception of rabbit-skin glue granules.

Method 1

70 g (2½ oz) of rabbit-skin granules should be soaked in 500 ml (1 pt) of cold water overnight, until soft.

Place the water and granules in a saucepan and heat slowly until all the granules have dissolved. Do not boil, as the water will evaporate

(cont'd from page 50)
The dark, rich gold, bronze powder was suspended in a polyurethane varnish and applied very thinly, followed when dry by the lemon gold bronze powder mixed with emulsion glaze to a thick paste. Nine different colours of acrylic paint were applied over the gold. It is interesting to note that the double action using different mediums with bronze powder creates a changing pattern. Viewed from certain positions in the room, the dark gold is almost invisible and the lemon gold shines brilliantly.

1 metre (1 yd) of fabric with a
    medium-coarse weave (natural
    fibres such as canvas, twill or old
    linen sheeting are recommended)
rabbit-skin glue granules
fine filler
artists' colour (oil or water)
polyurethane varnish
5–6 cm (2–3 in) household brushes
polythene sheet

making the glue stronger than necessary. When dissolved, the glue size will be a honey colour. While still hot, add 300 ml (½ pt) of tepid water and brush this briskly onto the cloth. A polythene sheet spread under the fabric will stop the glue penetrating into the work surface, and when the size is dry the cloth can be peeled away easily. Thoroughly soak the fabric in the size as it creates the bond between the fabric and the following layers. Leave the fabric to dry out completely – overnight or even longer.

Store any leftover size in the fridge. It will set to the consistency of a table jelly.

Take this remaining size in jelly form and warm it in a pan, being careful not to let it boil. Add another 300 ml (½ pt) of tepid water to it. Although diluted, it is still strong enough to bind with the fine filler, and to stick to the surface. Take the pan off the heat and let the glue cool down. While still warm, but not hot, add enough filler to the liquid to give the consistency of single cream. Stir continuously, trying to keep the mixture free of lumps and air bubbles.

Using a 5 cm (2 in) household paintbrush, apply the plaster and glue mixture onto the fabric, working this first coat well into the weave (on the polythene sheet again). Once covered, leave it to dry to the point where it has changed from a yeast colour to powdery white. Warm the size again if it has gone cold and apply a second coat; this time laying the mixture on lightly by filling the brush and floating it across the cloth. This application will take longer to dry and there is no telling an approximate time as the atmosphere and temperature of the work room affect the drying speed.

When this second coat has turned a dense chalky-white, coat again in the same way a further three times, allowing the fabric to dry between each application. After the final coat has been applied, leave again for at least twenty-four hours, until dry.

The now cardboard-like, stiff, plastered surface should be sealed with a polyurethane varnish. This can be done with a brush quite quickly, covering the porous surface evenly. Wait for this to dry before the next step.

Cracking: cracklure

Place the cloth on the edge of a hard surface, such as a work-top, bench, table or a shelf, and pull very quickly over the hard edge. This creates cracks in the plaster surface, but it does not break off. Repeat this in all directions, crossways, lengthways and diagonally. The cloth will start to become softer and easier to manage.

Now, the challenge begins and your artistry and imagination comes into play.

Distressing

Firstly, mix a small amount of artists' oil colour (preferably dark browns, greys, greens or reds) with white spirits or turpentine. This mixture should be thin enough to be soaked up by a piece of rag or paper towel.

Dip a rag or cloth into the mixture, and then rub it in circular movements over the surface of the varnished and cracked plaster cloth. The colour will sink into the cracks, leaving the surface varnish as it was. A brush can be used, but a cloth is still necessary to wipe off the excess.

The second stage is to mix two or three colours for the overall

Opposite: A school trunk in pine is transformed into an extraordinary leather-bound coffer with the aid of linen, glue and plaster. A little time may be spent on this technique, but the results show what transformations can be achieved with the simplest of materials.

colour of the leather. These should be diluted again with turpentine or white spirits and also applied with a cloth, but this time in a dabbing and pouncing way to give a mottled, broken surface. This layer of colour must remain transparent, so use this wash as thin as you can and build up the colour. You want every crack to show through. Waterproof inks can be used if you do not have time to wait for the oil washes to dry, although some of them have staining qualities and are difficult to handle on large areas where subtle tones are required.

Once you have the desired colour and effect, leave the wash to dry before applying your next sealer coat of matt or satin polyurethane varnish.

If a really authentic feel is required, once the sealer coat is dry the whole surface can be covered with wax polish. This gives a marvellous sheen in places, and the feel of wax polish is similar to the feel of old leather.

Method 2: gesso cracklure

In all ways, this method is far superior to the first, and has been practised for thousands of years. The ancient Egyptians used it quite extensively as part of their decorative art work. Gesso is used for gilding and there are as many recipes as individuals. Success with gesso takes hours of practice, but the end result of this method is very satisfying. Even a poor gesso mixture will not result in disaster. Problems will arise only if your patience runs out.

gesso
material of medium to coarse weave
  (natural fibre is preferable)
rabbit-skin glue granules
whiting
double-boiler
earthenware bowl or basin
wooden spoon
polythene sheet

Take 70 g (2½ oz) of rabbit-skin glue granules and put them to soak in 500 ml (1 pt) of water overnight, until soft.

Place the size in the top compartment of a double-boiler, or in an earthenware basin standing in a pan with water up to one third of the height of the basin. Keep the pan on the heat until the glue granules have melted (do not boil the glue size).

Take off the heat and add 300 ml (12 fl oz) of tepid water. This mixture can be applied to the fabric while warm. The fabric is then left to dry in exactly the same way as for the previous method (page 54).

The rabbit-skin size will set to a table jelly consistency and will have to be melted again in a double-boiler or basin and pan. As the glue size dissolves, add to it a further 300 ml (½ pt) of water. Then add enough whiting to make a mound in the centre of the pan. Leave a small peak breaking the surface. This should give you the right proportion of whiting to size.

Take a wooden spoon and very gently stir the whiting into the size. A single-cream consistency is best although a thickish milk will be quite acceptable in the case of cracklure. The thinner this mix, the more coats will be necessary to cover the weave of the cloth. On no account add more whiting to the mix after the initial stirring as it will form lumps and spoil the gesso. Never let the mixture get too hot or boil. Air bubbles and evaporation spoil a gesso enough to render the work unsuitable before you start.

A very clean, stiff-bristled household brush should be used to work the warm gesso into the sized canvas or cloth. Be quite firm when applying this coat as its success will be the making of the finished work. Rub the gesso well into the cloth, getting down into the fibres and knocking out any air that may be trapped in them.

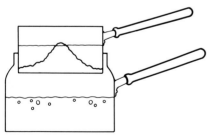

7 *A double-boiler is a necessary part of gesso-making. The quantity of whiting to size must be gauged correctly for good results.*

Absorbing this first coat, the cloth will dry quite quickly so be on the lookout for the tell-tale patches of dry gesso that will soon begin to appear. They will look powdery white. As this drying can create problems, the right moment must be chosen to apply the second coat. Air bubbles may show on the surface if it is too dry; if it is too wet, there is every possibility that your laying on the next coat will drag up the gesso from the first coat.

However small the surface you are applying gesso to, you must allow yourself at least half a day in the studio or at your work-bench in order that you can watch each drying stage. Other jobs can be done while you are waiting, but nothing is more important than your gessoed surface being caught at the right moment to apply the next coat.

Five layers will be enough for the cracklure effect, and each one should be layed on with a floating action after the initial first rubbing in. Use a soft, squirrel-hair brush with 3 cm (1½ in) long bristles. Usually used as fine lacquer brushes, they are ideal for floating on the layers of gesso.

Once dry, this gessoed surface can be sanded down with the finest wet and dry paper and its finish will be as soft to the touch as the finest silk. Treated to the same polyurethane sealer or the quick-drying, pale polish (see varnishes, page 121), the surface can be cracked by pulling it over a hard edge, as in the previous method (page 54). All steps from then on are the same; distressing to show the cracks as darker than the surface; and washes of thinned oil colour to simulate old leather.

Alternative ideas

To enhance your leather look-alike and give vent to your artistry and imagination, try using one of the following ideas to create a feeling of period.

Stencil work
Use acrylics or oil paints and stencil motifs.

Embossed leather
Mix bronze powder and fine filler in approximately 5 parts filler to 1 part bronze powder. Add to this enough polyurethane varnish to make a thin paste (similar in consistency to icing, when cake decorating). Snip the corner off a polythene bag (the tiniest cut will produce quite a big hole so do be careful). Fill the corner of the bag with the mixture and pipe the design of your choice with this paste over the surface.

fine filler
polyurethane varnish
polythene bag
bronze powder

Hand painting
Acrylic or oil paints can be used. The freedom of brush strokes and the look of the antique can be successfully combined to fool the keenest eye. Layers of paint followed by varnish tinted to a suitable, aged toffee colour, can be given a rub over with fine wire wool.

Metal leaf
Gold tooled leather can be simulated by this technique. First of all, design your border motif and draw it into the surface of the cracklure. Next, cover the design and surrounding area with talcum powder. This done, take a fine artists' brush and paint over the design

Japan gold size
fine artists' brush
talcum powder
Dutch metal leaf

with Japan gold size. The talcum powder helps to stop the gold size running into areas other than your design. When the gold size is almost dry, usually in two to five hours, depending on atmosphere, lay on the sheets of Dutch metal foil and pounce softly with a small wad of cotton-wool. Leave them to dry completely then remove excess Dutch metal by rubbing over the area with another cotton-wool pad.

CRACKLURE

To say there is beauty in the fine hair-line cracks of a surface is an example of beauty being in the eye of the beholder. To the Chinese, in their eastern wisdom, the cracking of a glaze on a pot or jar had such an appeal that it was looked upon as a feature to be duplicated rather than a surface that had been spoiled.

Japan has a similar version, although it is based rather more on a spiritual philosophy than a decorative pleasantry. A broken or damaged bowl, cup or vase took on a new and more cherished character because fate has dealt such a blow. The crack or repair was gilded over to show reverence to the soul of the object.

Worlds apart, the West only discovered the elegance and sympathetic quality of this effect in the eighteenth century.

Two fashionable interior designers called the Martin brothers, working at the French court, discovered a varnishing technique that created the illusion of the spider's-web lines found on old oil paintings. Panelling, furniture and objects were painted with romantic landscapes, lovers in arbours, and similar Watteauesque creations, and then varnished over. Cracked to an antiqued finish, the look became the rage. Within the next fifty years, Vernis Martin's, as the cracked varnish became known, travelled through Europe with speed and efficiency. Smaller items were treated with the same effect and trays, boxes and *objets d'art* found their way into a great many households for everyday use.

The technique of cracking a surface in this way is based upon the inter-action between two different mediums with different drying times: usually oil and water. An oil medium used for the first coat. This has a slow drying time, and quite a considerable amount of movement takes place. On to this surface when it is partly dry, a water-based, quick-drying solution is applied. As the double layer dries, the water-based surface splits and cracks with the movement of the oil base below.

For ease of application, there are ready-bottled solutions available for this instant cracking technique; success is guaranteed if you follow the manufacturer's instructions. As in the days of the Martin brothers, the French have perfected the best mixtures. Two solutions are provided: a varnish with an oil base, tinted to give an authentic, aged look for the first coat; and a water-based, glutinous liquid with a fast drying time, which is applied over the varnish.

The surface for cracklure must be non-porous. If the oil-based varnish sinks in on application, no cracks will appear on the surface when the second coat is applied. Make sure the piece of furniture or object is sealed to a non-porous finish, as in oil-based paints, varnishes or polyurethane.

To control the size of the cracks on the surface you are covering, you hold back the application of the second solution until the varnish

has reached a certain point. When the varnish is still slightly tacky to the touch, application of the water-based liquid will give large to medium-sized cracks. If the water-based coat is applied when the varnish is almost dry to the touch, minute eggshell-like cracks result. Do be careful not to over-handle the varnish when testing its drying state; finger-marks, once there, cannot be erased.

The problem most often encountered with the commercial, ready-made fluids is that the directions for drying times, stating thirty to forty minutes, can be completely wrong if the atmosphere you work in is damp, humid, or dry and hot. Therefore, do make a small test sample before you start to discover how long your base-coat has to be left before the second application is made, to produce the desired amount and size of cracks. When dry, the surface cracks will not be all that obvious. In certain cases, a hair-drier can be used to encourage the cracks to appear, but again it is necessary to test this beforehand. Too much hot air can lift the top surface; or cracks resembling mud-flats in full drought appear, and prevent the surface area cracking evenly. Remember also that, as the top surface is water-based, it is easily damaged.

Blackboard paint, given a golden chinoiserie design of the eighteenth century, covers the drawers of a pine chest. To complete the aged look a layer of cracklure covers the whole surface, which was then rubbed over with ground rotterstone.

An oil-coloured wash must be used to delve right down into the cracks to obtain the maximum effect and this is applied as follows.

5 cm (2 in) soft-hair brush
artists' oil colour (dark pigments or a
    strong colour)
turpentine or white spirits
mixing jar or container
soft rag

Mix the artists' oil colour of your choice with turpentine or white spirits until you have a watery glaze. Try to keep the colour as strong and as dark as possible as the cracks need to be seen. With the paintbrush, work over the surface, covering it evenly with the oil glaze until you can see the penetration of the colour into the cracks. Use a soft, clean cotton rag to take off the excess colour leaving only the cracks holding the glaze. For a really old, aged look, the rag can be pounced gently over the surface at this point leaving a fine mottled appearance. Leave the surface to dry overnight, or for a good eight hours. Seal it with a varnish of your choice.

Ceramics can also be treated with cracklure, as can glossy prints and magazine photographs.

6 PAINTING ON GLASS

There is no substitute for the magnificent substance we call glass, although its presence in our homes and in everyday life is taken very much for granted.

Regarded as precious and highly sought after in the beginning, glass has been worn as decoration, looked through, drunk from and played with. It has been used to make fire, and to create fantasies with its reflective qualities. The list of uses it has been put to over the centuries, all over the world, is a long one. And in modern times, despite the flood of new inventions carrying us towards the twenty-first century, glass is still important.

The earliest examples of painted glass date back to the ancient Egyptians in 1500 BC. Travelling the Middle East and Mediterranean, glass found varying styles of decoration used on its surface. Syria, Greece and Rome in particular created pieces which today hold pride of place in many a museum collection.

Three out of the four methods of painting on glass described in this chapter are based on past styles. Experimentation with these three techniques first should give you the necessary knowledge to start the fourth method with freedom and vitality.

STAINED GLASS EFFECT

Design the motif or picture on a sheet of cartridge paper the same size as the piece of glass. Decide where the leaded supports will be, as these are the first parts to be applied to the glass surface. When your design is complete, lay the cartridge paper down on a flat surface, face up, and place your sheet of glass on top of it. Place masking-tape over the edges of the glass for safety.

glass cut to size
glass paint or enamels (see page 124–25)
cartridge paper
bronze powder (silver)
emulsion glaze
polyurethane varnish
black acrylic paint
soft-hair paintbrush
polythene bag (small)

8 *Keep the lead joining-bars as realistic as possible by placing them in positions unrelated to the design motif.*

Mix the silver bronze powder, black acrylic paint, polyurethane varnish and emulsion glaze in the following proportions:

2 tablespoons bronze powder
1 tablespoon black acrylic paint
1 tablespoon emulsion glaze
1 tablespoon polyurethane varnish

Put this mixture into a clear polythene bag, snip off a small corner and use it like an icing-bag.

Apply to the glass, using your drawing underneath as a guide, to all the areas indicated as the lead bars that separate and hold the coloured glass.

Leave to dry overnight.

Using the paints or inks mixed to the colours of your choice, apply with light brush strokes to fill in the areas between the lead supports. Do not apply too much paint at any one time. A build-up of layer upon layer is much better than a thick, even-coloured coat. The colour value can be changed, too. A blue laid over a red will give a red-purple. A crimson laid over yellow will give a bright scarlet glow.

If you want to attempt the stained-glass effect of a church, seal the paint, once dry, with a polyurethane varnish in the area where you will draw in your subject.

When this has dried, use an Indian ink or black acrylic to paint the additional details onto the surface.

Seal this area again with polyurethane. When dry, additional layers of colour can be applied if necessary.

Always finish with a sealer coat of polyurethane.

Frame the glass if possible, as this prevents accidents and makes it easier to hang.

Common problems

Leaded bars crack and peel off:
This can be due to too much paint and not enough emulsion glaze in the mixture. Re-mix.

Streaks and bubbles in the paint:
This is the most common fault and is usually caused by working over an area with the paintbrush too often. Try to float the colour on rather than brushing it. Using a good quality, soft-hair brush which suits the size of the glass, or area, being coloured.

REVERSE METHOD

This is the most often seen of all glass-painting techniques. It can be treated as a fine art, or, at the other end of the scale, it can be primitive and wonderfully decorative. Some people find it a puzzling technique to master, but it is only a matter of careful observation. Details are painted first, and the subject is then built up by applications of colour, both transparent and matt. Taking the face as an example: eye lashes, lips, nostrils and hair would be painted first, followed by the pupils of the eyes, and shades and highlights on the face; next would come the whites of the eyes, the colouring of the skin, and the main bulk colour of the hair. In this way, layer upon layer of paint is built up to produce a quality of depth and feeling unlike anything that can be achieved on canvas or paper.

Remember that your painted image is trapped behind glass and will always be viewed through it.

Far right *Reverse painting*
9.1 *First paint in the fine details of the flower.*
9.2 *Shade the centre and middle of the petals.*
9.3 *Apply the main body colour over the entire design area, and seal it when dry with a coat of paint or varnish.*

Draw out your design on cartridge paper, or use a print or photograph if you wish to copy a motif. Prints are good to practise with as the colours and subject matter are already defined.

Lay your design or photograph on the flat surface and place the glass on top of it. Secure the glass in place with sticky tape to stop it moving about; a strip at top and bottom will be adequate.

Look at the details of your drawing or print and study exactly which part would be the closest to you if the subject were three-dimensional drawings.

Work with your finest brush and put these details onto the glass first.

When this is dry, choose the next group of surfaces. These will probably be shadows and highlights. Shadows will need to be transparent, and highlights will need to be white or off-white. Drawing inks are ideal for the transparent finishes as they dry quickly. Oil paints mixed with white spirits or turpentine work just as well but take longer to dry. The enamels used by model-makers are dense enough for the rest of the work.

Fill in the rest of the design step by step, waiting for the surfaces to dry properly before going over them.

When all the paint has been applied, seal it with a coat of polyurethane varnish. This can be sprayed on, to save disturbing the surface by brushing, and left to dry.

Common problems

Paint not staying on the surface:

When starting out, wipe over the surface of the glass with methylated spirits. This cleans the surface and removes any patches of grease or oil.

If paint starts to disperse (transparent inks are the most likely to do this), add a minute amount of methylated spirits to the ink.

Don't move the glass to inspect your paint as you may not get it back in the same position.

If you make a mistake, don't try to rub it off. Brush over the area lightly with a thin coat of solvent and blot with a cotton-wool pad to absorb the paint.

MIRROR-BACK AND *VERRE EGLAMISE*

Chinese mirror paintings command very high prices in salerooms. Their beauty lies in the exquisite delicacy of brush strokes, wonderful colour sense, and marvellous draughtsmanship. The technique used by the Chinese was an adaptation of working methods practised in Europe during the early eighteenth century. With little glass production in China, the East India Company and other merchant travellers took glass and mirrors to the Chinese for decoration. In the case of plain glass, the painting would be executed in oil or pigments mixed with a gum substance. They would then be transported back to Europe, and there be silvered with a mirror backing. If mirror was used to start with, the silver would be scraped away, leaving the shape and form of the design ready to receive paint and pigments.

The mirror look can be achieved at home with the use of metal foils. Brass and aluminium foils of extra-fine quality, known as Dutch metal or Shlag, are available. They are ideal for this work and inexpensive.

sheet of glass cut to size
cartridge paper or a print
acrylic paints
oil-based enamel paints (see page 124–25)
waterproof drawing inks
good selection of artists' brushes
flat working surface
polyurethane varnish

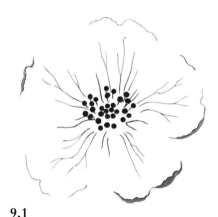

9.1

9.2

9.3

sheet of glass cut to size
cartridge paper or print
oil-based enamel paint
artists' oil paint
waterproof drawing ink
good selection of artists brushes (soft
  squirrel-hair)
one gelatine capsule, or a teaspoon of
  strong rabbit-skin size
one book of aluminium leaf (silver)
one book of brass leaf (gold)

Follow the instructions given for reverse painting, but do not seal with polyurethane.

Making sure all surfaces are dry, wipe over the remaining glass with a solution of 50 per cent methylated spirits and 50 per cent water, on a clean cloth. If your design is intricate, apply the solution with a brush and blot with a cloth to absorb the mixture. This should clean the surface.

To 150 ml (¼ pt) of hot water, add 1 capsule of gelatine or the rabbit-skin size. Let this dissolve completely, and then add 1 teaspoon of methylated spirits.

With a soft brush, float sufficient size onto the surface of the glass to cover it with a thin film.

Lift up a square of metal foil with your finger tips, being careful not to tear it, and place it gently on the film.

If the glass is larger than 20 cm (8 in) square, it will be difficult to cover the surface with metal foil at one time. If this is the case, divide the square into 20 cm (8 in) squares and cover one at a time with the film of size. Overlap each square a little as this helps cover up any discrepancies in the laying of the metal.

Once the whole surface has been covered and the water has evaporated sufficiently not to run or cause the foil to split, take a cotton-wool swab and press very gently over the surface of the foil. Great care must be taken not to pull at the metal as in this fragile state breaks, no matter how small, will show on the glass when it is reversed.

Leave this surface to dry completely (approximately two to three hours).

Tips for antique effects

Mix 50 per cent raw umber and 50 per cent black waterproof ink. Add a small amount of silver-bronze powder and spray with a diffuser onto the glass after painting but before laying the metal leaf. This fine speckled effect makes the mirror look mysteriously grey and aged. Leave it to dry before applying the water size.

Dip a piece of kitchen roll into raw umber or sepia waterproof ink and blot over the surface of the glass to be covered with foil. The effect created by this will appear to have been caused by years of damp penetrating the back surface of the glass.

When the metal has been applied and is dry, rub over the surface lightly with a cotton-wool swab. The smallest hair lines will appear without too much pressure. For a very distressed finish, a muslin or similar cloth can be used. With a soft brush dipped into a dark brown wood stain (an oil-based stain is the best for this purpose) cover the surface of the metal. The stain will bleed into the fine cracks giving an overall aged appearance.

EXPERIMENTAL

Completely free of any influences from the past, the glass paintings described here are ideas for the adventurous to try out without feeling tied down to a set technique. Do not be shy about taking the first steps. Glass is not affected by paint in any way. Mistakes can soon be rectified by scraping the painted mishap off and starting again. The methods described give results in a very short space of time, and can transform plain glass into a stylish marbled mirror.

Onto a sheet of glass lay an oil glaze using one of the techniques described in Chapter 2. Ragging, bagging, or clouding will work well, especially if the pigment chosen is transparent: for example, crimson or ultramarine. Bronze powders thrown into the glaze look good too. Let this surface dry out completely then spray over it with a cellulose spray-paint in a contrasting colour. A metallic spray can be used if you want a glittering, mirror-like background. Once this has dried, spray again with a clear polyurethane to seal the backing, and let this dry also. This treatment on a badly-scratched coffee-table top, or glass panel doors in a cupboard or cabinet, will spruce up the glass to look ten times better.

Masking-tape applied in strips, or diagonally to form squares or diamonds, will add a new dimension to the same effect, putting pattern within pattern.

A motif stencilled with cellulose car-spray onto a surface that has been given an oil glaze or contrasting coloured spray, can be very effective.

French enamel varnish and methylated spirits, used as in the tortoise-shell technique described on page 95, can be adapted for glass. Dutch metal or aluminium foil laid behind the varnish when it has dried gives a mirrored brilliance through the umber and amber depths.

The peacock colours of green, blue and bronze look fantastic when applied to glass.

7 DECOUPAGE
(PAPER CUTS)

In the seventeeth century, the merchant ships of the large trading companies brought great quantities of Chinese and Japanese lacquerware into the best-known European ports. Lacquerware became fashionable to the point of lacquer-mania, and demand soon outstripped supply. English cabinet-makers, furious that their livelihood was under threat from these imported items of furniture and objects, started to produce their own versions of lacquerware. In France and Italy, craftsmen ready to jump on the fashion-conscious band-wagon followed suit. The latter, with Venice as the port and centre of a flourishing artists' community, developed a technique for decorating furniture using engravings coloured by hand and sealed by many coats of varnish. This *lacche povere* or 'poor man's lacquer' was a great success, and in its turn spread through Europe.

With a name-change in France to découpage, the poor man's lacquer was taken up as a genteel pastime; something for the ladies to do to while away the afternoon hours, snipping gracefully at flower prints and caring meticulously about the placing of these delicate cuttings. Examples of their labours are totally enchanting.

In Victorian England, découpage received a new lease of life. The fruits of numerous scissor cuts can still be found in many an antique shop. Screens were a favourite surface to decorate, although they were perhaps not as beautifully executed as the Italian or French work, for by Victorian times, the fashion for chinoiserie and frivolity had been superceded by a heavier, denser decorative effect.

Découpage is perhaps one of the simplest and least expensive of all decorative techniques. Prints, papers, colour supplements: all are within easy reach at little or no expense. What matters most is imagination and ingenuity. Don't fall into the trap of cutting out pretty pictures and sticking them down like postage stamps on an envelope. The real joy of this effect is in creating, from an object or piece of furniture that lacks style and character, a product of your own artistry and a personal statement of your talents. Arrange colours and shapes so that they give the impression of space or time, maybe even perspective. Going back to the postage stamp, even these can be used to effect. A box covered with used postage stamps and pieces of gold doylie can look like an enamelled and jewelled casket, although that is a very simple way of using this technique.

Start with an item that is not too big; or even start by clipping out pictures that interest you from magazines, newspapers, and so on, and put them in a folder until you find an object you want to decorate. A collection of scraps like this will help you choose a theme, or provide a motive for building up certain picture effects. Ideal places to look for material are charity shops selling bundles of glossy magazines for a few pence, old calendars, gardening catalogues, and wrapping papers from birthday and Christmas time. Old maps can make wonderful border designs if quantity is needed.

When purchased this pine crocquet chest was covered with four different-coloured layers of gloss paint. Stripped and sanded, it awaits new layers of primer/sealer, undercoat and two coats of creamy white, oil-based, mid-sheen paint.

Definitely leaning towards the ecclesiastical, the chest is decorated with prints of saints placed among architectural niches built up from sale-room catalogues, including Wedgewood plates, Fabergé binoculars, saltcellars and jewellery, linked with wreaths of laurel leaves painted with acrylic paint in dark ochre and grey.

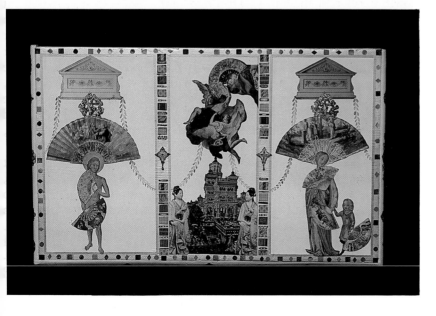

The chest top showing an assortment of print motifs, the main two sets being fire-place mounts and Spanish fans. Japanese figures invite the eye to enter a Florentine palace as angels view the scene from a cloudy heaven. Four coats of polyurethane were applied on top of this to protect the prints and paint.

As many pictures from magazines have print on the reverse side, it is advisable to test a sample, coating it with the varnish of your choice. Paper, being porous, can turn transparent when varnish is applied, and print showing through to the top surface would certainly spoil the image.

Surface preparation

Any firm surface will take découpage. Clean the surface thoroughly before starting work on it, as glue will not adhere to a dirty surface. If you wish to change the background colour of the object, car-spray covers most surfaces and will dry quickly. Emulsion paint would be cheaper but it cannot be applied to plastic or high-gloss surfaces. Acrylic paints will give a reasonably good cover, although they are expensive to use in quantity. Model-makers' enamel paints are excellent for small objects and dry in approximately six hours. Stripped wood can be stained or, for an unusual bleached look, a solution of 50 per cent emulsion paint in palest blue-grey and 50 per cent water can be brushed on, left to dry, then lightly rubbed over with fine wire wool. The paint, being diluted, sinks into the wood but leaves the grain showing through.

PVA fixative, which comes in spray cans, prevents any varnish sinking into the surface. Do use it if possible.

scalpel or sharp scissors (both if possible)
prints, magazines, scraps of paper
pencil
paste brush and suitable paste (see pages 124–25), but not wallpaper paste
varnish (polyurethane)
varnish brush
white spirits
extras: artists' oil paint and brushes for decoration around the borders, to give a livelier look to your work.

It can be difficult to imagine the effect of a finished object. With a jigsaw puzzle, every piece has its right place; with découpage, the end result lies entirely in your hands and eyes.

If you cut a piece of plain paper to the size and shape of the object you are going to decorate, and work on it as an artist works on a canvas, it will help you achieve the best results. Accidental composition can give novel twists you perhaps had not thought of.

All edges must be cut cleanly. Try to keep joins edge-to-edge rather than overlapping. If curves are difficult or on the small side, turn the paper in towards the scissors, or better still, use a scalpel blade.

To get a clear impression of your creation while still being able to alter the composition, use a very light, spray adhesive. With it, the paper can be lifted and re-positioned many times over. Used with care and in conjunction with a heavier spray adhesive for the actual découpage work, it will enable you to see the design laid flat.

Once the design is to your liking, paste or glue the paper prints onto the piece itself. Don't let adhesive cover any part of the front of the paper. Use the adhesive sparingly if it has a water base. Too much paste can make the paper bubble, which will spoil the finished effect. A small wallpaper roller can help to eliminate bubbles.

Make sure all the edges of the paper are well and truly stuck down. Fine cuttings, such as flower stems and architectural details, can be problematical. A small artists' brush with a little paste on it should be kept at hand for these areas.

Leave the paper to dry out at room temperature before varnishing.

Seal the surface with a PVA fixative. This will prevent any transparent areas developing.

Varnishing

Try to keep a brush specially for varnishing. A household paintbrush is fine, although a little on the heavy side. Good varnish brushes are worth looking after and many years of service can be had from one so long as you don't use it for any other purpose.

Polyurethane varnish, once applied, is virtually indestructible under normal circumstances. Water and spirits don't have much effect on the surface, and heat and cold do little to harm its structure. Two to five coats of this varnish, with a day or so in between each application, should build up a surface that will last for generations to come.

Float the varnish on, working from the centre of the outside edge outwards towards the top and bottom (figs. 10.1 and 2).

Work the brush through this in the opposite direction, being careful not to pull too much from any one area (fig. 10.3).

Repeat this in strips, working across the piece until completed.

Before each application of varnish, a light rub down with the finest of wire wools is advisable. This helps to key in the additional coat and give greater transparency to the varnish itself.

To give an antique patina to the surface varnish, rub down with wire wool and then apply a tinted wax polish. Other effects, such as cracklure (see page 58–60), add a very distinctive look.

Alternative ideas

Combine paper cut-outs with painted *trompe l'oeil*. Perspective can be created by painting in shadows and highlights around the cut-outs to produce a three-dimensional effect.

Try metallic papers or transparent cellulose papers over the top of coloured paper to duplicate the look of gold, silver, enamel, jewels, and so on.

Thin slithers of mother-of-pearl (see page 59) placed between the paper shapes can look very authentic and beautiful on a black base.

10 *Varnishing*

8 MARBLING

A survey of the many ways in which man has duplicated the look of marble would itself fill a book. Fantasies of veining and colours undulating as if moved by a timeless rhythm, have created a legacy of painted marbles spanning four thousand years.

The creation of marble is a marriage of heat and pressure. Minerals and stones fusing and crystallizing over millions of years with the changing earth. As eruptions altered the strata and surface of the land, so in time the cavities and cracks were filled in and the layers pressed down, creating the thousands of types of marble that are known today.

A knowledge of the real stone is obviously an advantage when you are trying to re-create it in paint, so do take every opportunity to study the type of marble you are imitating. You do not have to go far for this. A visit to the nearest town will produce at least two or three versions of this grand rock as it covers offices, shops and graves alike.

Four methods of marbling are described in this chapter: oil glaze marbling, watercolour on an oil base (resist solvent method), oil colour on a water base, and moss marbling.

The first two methods can be used on all surfaces. The surface being marbled should first be prepared according to the instructions given in Chapter 1.

The second two methods are for producing marbled papers, and moss marbling can also be used on fabrics such as cotton, linen, calico and silk. In each case, a size mixture is used, either rabbit-skin size or Carragheen moss size. Spots of colour are dropped onto the surface of the size and worked to produce patterns, and the paper (or fabric) is then floated on the surface to absorb the colour.

Marbled papers can be used to cover lampshades and bases, desk equipment, note-books, gift boxes and numerous small objects. There is no reason why they should not also be used on larger areas, such as furniture and walls. A dining-table top made from the cheapest chipboard, given two coats of undercoat to seal the surface, then applied with cut-out shapes of marbled paper and varnished, would look marvellous. Paper will cut easily, adhere to most surfaces with the correct paste, and, if treated with care, will have a life-span of many, many years.

Experiment with each of the methods described here to discover the qualities of that particular medium. The success of marbling is in the eye of the artist, not necessarily that of the beholder. With this in mind, take up the brushes and enjoy the experience.

OIL GLAZE MARBLING

Surface preparation
An oil base-paint is used for all oil-based marbling techniques. See Chapter 1 for instructions on surface preparation. As for the choice of a base colour: serpentine or black and gold marble would go on a black background, worked in with a lighter colour; porphyry on a red or green background; and sienna on a cream base. For a fantasy

marble to suit a particular decorative scheme the base can be any colour.

Tools

Oil glaze marbling is not always done with brushes. For centuries, goose feathers have been used successfully as veining tools. Several everyday items found about the house can be used: newspapers, polythene bags, sponges, old rags, and even vegetables. The results produced with these can be realistic or fantastic, yet always stay within the realms of marbling.

Goose feathers Used to give a vein of movement and character. Drawn down the marble and flipped slightly from side to side, the width of line alters considerably.

Goose brush A long-haired brush that holds quite a lot of paint. This brush for veining is of medium thickness but swivelled in the fingers or given a nervous twist, it achieves a line of differing width and quality.

Badger-hair softener One of the most expensive brushes to buy, the beginner will find this brush beautiful to use. The effect of softening the edges of a vein and blending the marble into a liquid delicacy can make the artist's translation a reality.

Newspaper Breaks in a marble surface stand out quite strongly. A piece of screwed-up newspaper imitates these lines well. Folded into 3 cm (1½ in) strips, it can be drawn across a wet glaze to indicate strata flow. As newsprint is black, a certain amount comes off as you work with it. This happy accident results in a grey that becomes an extra colour on your marble. If you do not want the surface discoloured in this way, a piece of folded cartridge paper will duplicate the same strata effect.

Polythene bags (heavy-duty polythene) Breccia marble is well known for containing small rocks and pebbles of different sizes and colours. A background glaze covered with a loosely scrunched-up polythene bag placed at random, then lifted off will give the marble a definite rock-like formation.

Lightweight polythene The tissue thin quality of this polythene closely bunched up and pounced over a dark glaze that has been applied to a light surface creates the appearance of minute, faceted veins which happen on the base of serpentine marbles.

Sponges Natural sea sponges with various sized holes are interesting when placed on passages of marbling, giving an effect of gradual colour change and depth. This is the most noticeable feature of sponging. A dark glaze over a light background takes on a granite-like look.

Old rags A surface rubbed haphazardly with old rags is the usual starting point for most marbles except porphyry or granite. Scrubbed in some places and pounced in others, a cloudy depth of colour is left on the wall or surface.

Vegetables For duplicating the remains of fossils found in a group of marbles known as fossilferrous, vegetables come into their own in the world of decorative art. It is amazing what you can do with a carrot, or for that matter a potato, parsnip and half an onion. These vegetables should be cut in half and wiped with a cloth. They can create the look of fish, insects and primitive life forms from millions of years ago.

Brushes Keep as many different types to hand as possible. Sawn-off household paintbrushes can be used with white spirits to splatter over a surface glaze, leaving flecks and spots of the base colour showing through. Stencil brushes pounced over a glazed surface can create an attractive effect before veins are added. You will soon discover which brushes suit your own way of marbling.

A practice piece of veined marbling

Mix enough glaze in proportion to white spirits needed to cover the surface you are to work on. For example:

1 tablespoon of glaze to cover 2 sq m (2 sq yd)
300 ml (½ pt) white spirits

artists' oil paint
scumble glaze or home-made glazing
   liquid (page 12)
white spirits
brushes for glaze application
artists' brushes for veining
cloths
paper towels
jars for mixing colours
pot or bucket for mixing glaze

Take half the glaze mixture and add a teaspoon of artists' oil colour mixed to the major body colour of the marble you have chosen.

Mix thoroughly with a paint brush.

Paint this all over the piece you intend to marble and aim for a random colour, changed in certain areas. If you brush this glaze on too evenly, it will mean more work later on. (See Clouding, pages 25–26, for an alternative way of applying paint.)

Allow this to dry for an hour. The turpentine substitute will evaporate during this time leaving the glaze and paint slightly sticky but manageable.

Take a soft rag and rub over the glaze lightly. Remove some areas right back to the base colour and leave other parts almost untouched. Use a rag to blot areas where brush strokes show as lines.

Take the same glaze again and working with an artist's brush, mix in a little more of the oil colour. This darker glaze is applied as a background to the veins. A nervous directional line of approximately 2–4 cm (1–2 in) in width is best.

Leave for fifteen minutes; then blend it into the glaze already applied with a stippling motion. A brush or a sponge can be used for this job.

Pour a small amount of the original glaze and spirit mixture into a saucer or container and add the colour you have chosen for the veins of the marble, little by little, until you have a creamy liquid. It should not be too wet, or the veins may become too transparent or run in drips down the surface.

Using a long-haired brush (goose or similar), take up the colour and roll the brush in the direction of the last application over the surface with staccato movements. Try to keep the brush on the surface all the time for these first major veins.

Using the badger-hair softener, blend out one side of the vein leaving a sharp edge on the opposite side. The background will usually dictate where the veins should be placed but if you have difficulty in finding the right areas, stand back and take a look from a distance.

A smaller, finer artists' brush can be used for laying in very fine veins. These can cross in the opposite direction from the veins already applied. Try to avoid forming squares, circles or arches. Elongated diamond shapes with blended edges work well, as do irregular stone-like shapes.

Blend in the fine veins, and add still finer veins in a contrast colour or white. The tip of a brush that has been skimmed across a tube of

A fire-place corner showing in close-up the marbled veins and islands associated with the Italian Sienna marble.

11.1 *Apply the background colour for the marble veins directionally.*

11.2 *Stipple lightly to blend with the base colour already on the wall.*

11.3 *Create irregular veining by using a long-haired artists' brush.*

11.4 *Brush over one edge of the vein with a badger-softener to give the qualities of depth and flow inherent in most Sienna marbles.*

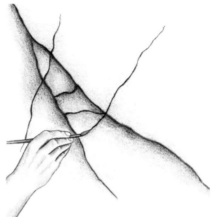

11.5 *Smaller veins can be applied at this stage of the work, but avoid creating shapes that look square or circular.*

11.6 *Using a soft cloth wrapped around the index finger, remove small islands of glaze all the way back to the base coat.*

artists' colour can give a marvellous intensity to some areas of veining.

With a rag soaked in white spirits, wrapped around the index finger, lift out small islands of paint to go right back to the base colour. These give great depth.

A light blending over the whole surface can be done now, but do stand back from the work and view it. Veins may look heavy enough when working close up, but they could disappear at two paces.

On completion, leave the surface for at least twelve hours before checking whether it is ready to varnish. Atmosphere plays its part with this technique as with all the oil glazes in this book.

Seal with a clear matt or semi-matt varnish, unless you want a brilliant, reflective, glass-like look (not recommended unless the wall or object is perfectly smooth).

artists' oil paints (white, paynes grey,
   raw umber, yellow ochre, burnt
   sienna)
scumble glaze or home-made glazing
   liquid (see page 12)
white spirits
three 5 or 6 cm (2 or 2½ in)
   paintbrushes
newspaper folded into strips
   12 × 3 cm (5 × 1½ in)
paper towels
three jam jars
basin or bowl

12.2

12.3

12.4

Travertine marble (strata effect)

Base colour: off-white to cream, cream or stone are best.

In a basin or bowl, mix enough scumble glaze and white spirits or home-made glazing liquid to cover the area or object you want to marble (see page 72).

Working with colours, in separate jars, mix three different hues of beige:

   a pink beige – white, burnt sienna and a dot of raw umber;
   a grey brown beige – white, raw umber and a dot of paynes grey;
   a yellow beige – white, raw umber and yellow ochre.

Try to keep them light. The darkest beige should be just darker than milky coffee.

Add an equal amount of glaze liquid gradually to each, until you have a creamy liquid; not too wet as the paint will run down the wall or object and you will be left with a denser coat of colour at the bottom than at the top.

When thoroughly mixed, load one brush at a time and work in uneven strips from top to bottom of the surface. Don't break the line as a strata effect is the basis of this marbling method. Leave gaps of the base colour showing if possible.

An area of 2 × 3 m (6 × 9 ft) can be covered and remain workable. The drying time does not matter too much as you can apply a further strip of glaze up to three or four hours after commencing work.

When you have covered the whole of the surface with these stripes of beige, take the folded newspaper, place it on its edge and work down each stripe with a tapping motion from side to side. Aim for a herring-bone effect.

Keeping the newspaper folded, take two or three strips out of every ten, running down from top to bottom in one continuous movement using the tip only. Small jerky movements can give the effect of a gentle flow, and in certain areas a slight bulging outwards of the veins can look very authentic.

12.1

By placing the paper flat onto the surface then lifting off straight away, speckles of colour and newsprint will be left that give depth and added interest to the lined look of travatine.

Leave to dry for at least a day. Then seal with semi-matt varnish.

Alternative ideas

This simple technique can be made really remarkable and convincing on a large scale if the wall or panel being decorated is split into blocks. A pencil line or crayon in a mid-grey can work as a joining line for each slab. Although it is a longer process, this method makes a large area more manageable, especially if you are working on your own.

Fantasy travertine A bold statement of colour looks superb in this simple technique. Shades of claret red on a scarlet background give the feel of tree bark illuminated by a camp fire. Three greens on an ochre ground creates a snake skin effect. Shades of ultramarine blue give an underwater atmosphere when used over a brilliant green. Try out examples of this effect on small panels, and experiment with ways of using the folded paper to give added texture.

Porphyry and granite (speckle effect)

This is a group of fine, mottled rocks with few, or no veins.

Traditional colours for this type of stone are dark red to purple, silver grey and green, brown and salmon pink with black and white. Any colour combination can be used when experimenting, although the best results are those that stay within the realms of the real rock. *Base colour*: this can be any colour, depending on the decorative scheme you are working towards.

In a basin, mix enough scumble glaze and white spirits to cover the area you wish to work on.

Using artists' oil colour, mix in separate jars three or four shades of your chosen colour.

Add to these an equal amount of glaze or glazing liquid and mix until you have a fine, creamy liquid; but not too creamy or you will end up with a raised, spotty surface.

Take the glaze you consider to have the overall colour value of the finished work and brush it over the whole surface.

Once covered, damp down the sea sponge to enlarge the holes and wipe on a piece of kitchen roll to remove any excess moisture.

Blot the sponge over the entire glaze to produce a mottled effect.

artists' oil paint
scumble glaze or home-made glazing
  liquid (see page 12)
white spirits
natural sea-sponge
three or four jam jars
bowl for mixing glaze if using
  scumble and white spirits
5 cm (2 in) household paintbrush
30 cm (12 in) length of 5 × 2 cm
  (2 × 1 in) wood
stencil brush, or brush with bristle cut
  down to 2 cm (1 in) in length

Granite.

Opposite *Travertine marble*
12.1 *Irregularity of line and colour application is a must for this marble effect to succeed.*
12.2 *Working with folded newspaper, blot some of the stripes with a criss-cross tapping movement.*
12.3 *Folded paper drawn down the glaze from ceiling to floor will give the appearance of strata flow.*
12.4 *Lay the paper flat to the surface glaze, press down and lift off.*

Load the 5 cm (2 in) household paintbrush and, starting with the darkest colour or shade first, take the length of wood in one hand and gently tap the brush against its side, holding it approximately 5–7 cm (2–3 in) away and covering the whole surface evenly.

Follow with the other colours until you have a build-up of tiny spots covering the whole surface.

The surface can be worked into if faults occur, using a stencil brush or a household paintbrush with stiff bristles in a stippling movement. Large blobs of paint can be dispersed by blotting with a paper towel. If you would like to break up the surface even more, take white spirits onto a stencil brush and flick the bristles over it with your fingers. This action separates the glaze and shows the base colour. The depth that this gives is well worth the effort.

Wait until the glaze has dried properly; with this method it can be one or two days, depending on how much glaze you have applied.

For a quicker version of this porphyry look, see moss marbling techniques (page 83).

You may want to give this imitation stone a very glossy finish. If so, apply four or five coats of varnish, sanding down after the third and fourth coats to achieve the perfect illusion of polished stone. If the surface is rather granular to the touch, a semi-matt varnish would be the wisest choice.

Alternative ideas
Mask off a design, like simple geometrical shapes, and use two or three contrasting colours for each area. Table-tops and panels have been executed in this way with real porphyry.

Bronze powder mixed with one of the glaze applications creates a crystallized glitter sometimes seen in the true stone.

Fossilferrous
The idea that a parsnip can be turned into a million-year-old shellfish takes some imagining. The same applies to potatoes, onions and carrots. However, this way of duplicating a particular type of marble gives you a freedom of expression that can be taken as seriously or light-heartedly as you want. A glance through a natural history book will set you on the right track for developing these centipedes and sea-snail characteristics.
Base colour: White or just off-white are best.

artists' oil paint (only one colour is necessary – suitable colours are: black, dark green, raw umber, or middle Indian red)
scumble glaze or home-made glazing liquid (see page 12)
white spirits
polythene bag (fine quality)
5 cm (2 in) paintbrush
rags or paper towels
cocktail sticks or toothpicks
container for glaze
vegetables of choice

Mix the oil colour and glaze or glazing liquid to the amount needed for the piece you are working on (see page 72).

Once thoroughly mixed, apply an even coat all over the surface using a 5 cm (2 in) paintbrush.

Crunch up the thin polythene bag in the hand and work over the whole surface with this. Fine lines of the base coat should show through at different angles and directions.

Cut the vegetables in half: carrots lengthwise, onions crossways. Skewer them with cocktail sticks from the back so that you can pick them up and put them down with ease.

Blot the vegetable on a rag or paper towel and apply it to the wet glaze surface. Press down as hard as you can. It does not matter if you slip from side to side a little as this accidental movement can create a very convincing fossil shape.

Lift off the vegetable and work into the shape you have made with

Fossilferrous.

the end of another cocktail stick. This can be time consuming. You should aim to create a skeletal form resembling the creature that lived all those years ago.

A splattering of white spirits from the bristle ends of a brush will help to simulate the minuscule crustacea, and a cotton-wool swab attached to the end of an artists' paintbrush handle and dipped in white spirits will produce many a blurred fossil fantasy.

Leave to dry for at least twenty-four hours before varnishing. Seal with a semi-matt varnish.

Alternative ideas
Use grasses and leaves instead of vegetables. Ferns are found in fossil form all over the world. These could look wonderfully decorative in this context. A small roller will come in handy for getting a good impression on the glaze.

WATERCOLOUR ON AN OIL BASE (RESIST SOLVENT METHOD)

The key components in this form of marbling are: (a) a catalyst to make the water-based paint cling to the oil-based surface; and (b) a solvent to break the surface of the watercolour, leaving areas of the base colour showing through. If this sounds too complex and scientific, one attempt will prove just how simple and easy this technique is.

Refer to Chapter 1 for details of surface preparation. Horizontal, flat surfaces are the easiest to work on, although small areas on a vertical plane can be marbled with care.

Fill a jam jar with enough water to cover the total area of the piece to be marbled.

To this add two or three gouache colours, a little at a time, to produce the overall body colour of the finished marble (see page 78–9 for suggested colour mixes). Stir thoroughly. Colours made up in this way tend to separate well, giving depth to the look of the piece.

The mixture should be heavily coloured; watery rather than a

artists' gouache watercolour paint
5 cm (2 in) soft-haired, flat paintbrush
assortment of artists' soft-haired
  brushes (flat)
methylated spirits
washing-up liquid
stiff bristle brush
water
jam jars for mixing paint

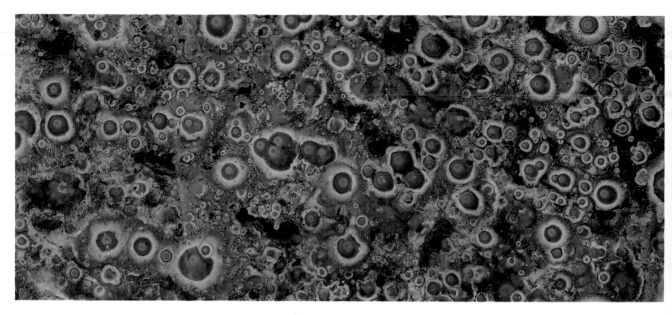

Marble: watercolour on an oil base.

A lamp-base given a new look. Over a black base, a mixture of rose pink gouache and lemon gold bronze powder was applied, followed by a splattering with methylated spirits. Once dry, the entire base was sealed with polyurethane spray varnish.

single-cream consistency. Add to this a teaspoon of washing-up liquid per half jam jar of mixture.

Fill a jam jar with methylated spirits and keep the selection of artists' brushes to hand. For a simple splatter look, a chopped-off household paintbrush with hard bristles works well.

Load the 5 cm (2 in) soft-haired paintbrush with paint mixture. Work as quickly as possible to cover the surface being marbled. If the paint dries on any part of the work, you will have to start again.

Dip the widest and flattest of the artists' brushes into the methylated spirits, and draw it lightly across the painted surface, from one side to the other or diagonally. Watch the paint when it comes in contact with the spirits.

Different-sized brushes can be used to make smaller veins. Try to avoid working over the surface too much.

Once you have covered the area with these fine lines to produce a strata type of marbling, dip a stiff-bristled brush into the methylated spirits and flick a light spray onto selected parts of the work. These break the monotony of the lined strata and create patches of colour that vary in intensity.

Leave it to dry completely and then varnish to seal the surface.

Alternative ideas

No artists' paintbrushes need be used for a bird's-eye speckle. Taking a stencil brush dipped into the methylated spirits, flick it evenly over the entire surface. This should result in small dots encircled by a ring of lighter colour.

For a fossil look, use a brush loaded with methylated spirits and lash it across the paper from a height of approximately 30 cm (12 in).

Mix bronze powder with the methylated spirits and flick this mixture into the paint. The bands of metallic powder look wonderful against dark or intense colours such as Prussian blue, indigo, viridian and red ochre.

Suggested colour mixes for gouache paint

Napoleon marble Equal parts of oxide of chromium, ultramarine and alizarin crimson over a white base.

Sienna Equal parts of Naples yellow, raw sienna and raw umber over a cream base.
Traventine 1 part raw umber and 2 parts white over a white base.
King's red 2 parts red ochre and 1 part Chinese orange over a white base.
Serpentine Equal parts of oxide of chromium, viridian and black over a white base.

The colours to avoid are the high-staining colours that tend to be fugitive. Try to stay with those colours that are extremely permanent, or durable to a high degree.

OIL COLOUR ON A WATER BASE

The beauty of this method of marbling lies in the creation of a free, flowing pattern that has no set rules in colour or design, although certain patterns are more common, such as those of book end-papers. This is an inexpensive marbling technique, and the few materials that are needed can be very easily handled. The results are almost instantaneous, and each one is different from the others.

Fine white or tinted paper is used. A slightly absorbent paper that is not too thick or too thin, is best. Avoid glossy paper as the paint may not adhere to it properly. Try out different papers until you find one that you like.

Mix 70 g (2½ oz) of rabbit-skin size with 500 ml (1 pt) of water and leave overnight to soak. The following day, heat this in a pan until all the size has dissolved. Remove from the heat and add another 500 ml (1 pt) of cold water.

This size should keep in a refrigerator for at least a month. If you are marbling in the bath, you may need this amount for the quantity of water. If you are covering only two or three sheets of paper, the sachet of gelatine as used in cooking will be more appropriate. Read the directions before commencing work.

Colour mixing: Using as many jam jars as you want colours on your marbled paper, pour into each enough white spirits to cover the bottom to a height of 1 cm (½ in). To this add a squeeze of artists' oil colour measuring approximately 5 cm (2 in) in length. Mix thoroughly to a single-cream consistency.

Using 70 g (2½ fl oz) of size to every litre (2 pt) of warm water, fill the tray to a depth of 3 cm (1½ in). If using the bath, add the size accordingly, but you will need to measure the quantity of water flowing into the bath to get the mixture right.

Fill an artists' brush with colour and let it drip onto the surface of the size. Each spot should float and spread to approximately twice its original size. If it spreads in a vast circle, your colour mixture is too thin. Therefore add more oil colour. If it drops to the bottom, add a little more white spirits.

Using a different brush for each colour, test each one to make sure you have the right consistency.

Cover the whole surface of the size with spots of colour.

Using cocktail sticks or any other fine-pointed tool, draw out the circles of colour into swirling spirals. Run across the surface diagonally to produce energetic flows of colour into colour. Every movement of the stick will bring about a change in the surface.

If you want to add more spots, keep the movement as bold as

rabbit-skin size, or gelatine
flat tray or large sink (24 × 18 in) this
    will take A 2 paper
jam jars
paper
cocktail sticks and paintbrushes
oil colours
white spirits
newspaper for cleaning the surface of
    the size

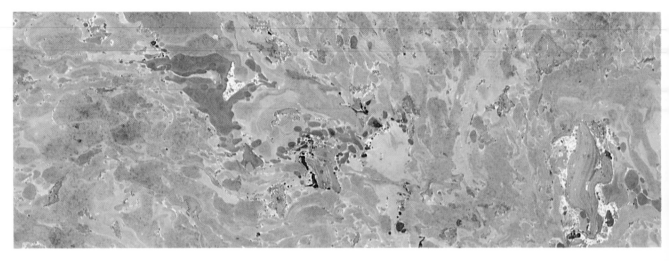

Marble: oil colour on a water base.

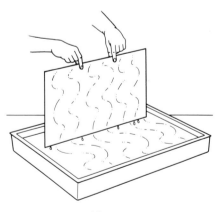

13 *Using a marbling tray.*

possible, and the contrast as defined as you can in certain areas. Too much stick-work will produce a finely speckled surface that lacks character.

When satisfied with your paintwork, take a sheet of paper by both sides, slightly bending its centre towards the paint. Position it centrally over the tray and let it roll quickly from the middle to the outsides in one smooth action. The paper will float on the surface and absorb the colour.

Lift one edge of the paper gently from the tray with both hands and hold it over the container until most of the excess size has drained away.

Place it on a sheet of newspaper to dry out. If it buckles, a warm iron, when it is completely dry, will flatten it out.

Take a strip of folded newspaper and skim the surface of the size to pick up any oil colour that has not been absorbed. This must be done on completion of each piece of paper or your marbling will start to look very messy.

Alternative ideas

Mix a little bronze powder with the oil paint and white spirits. Large areas do not look particularly effective, but a hint of lustre around the edges of a flat colour adds a special quality.

Wood dyes (spirit based): these transparent dyes can be used straight from the tin onto the size in the same way as oil colour. The rather soupy colours are ideal for achieving a mellow, antique effect.

MOSS MARBLING

Carragheen moss, sold in health and vegetarian food stores, is used as a base for this marbling process. The moss is, in fact, a seaweed from Ireland with the power to suspend colours to such an extent that their manipulation can be controlled to the millimetre. Another feature of this form of base size is that no colour, once laid, merges with another. This helps to give sharp contrast to the smallest details, and prevents the overall appearance from looking grey or muddy.

The method calls for extensive preparation before marbling can begin. Both the size and the colours have to be specially mixed, and the surface to be marbled must be treated with allum mordant, which acts as a colour fixative.

Preparation of size

Place 30 g (1 oz) of moss in a saucepan and cover with 1 litre (2 pt) of water.

Bring it to the boil slowly and continue to boil for four minutes, stirring continuously.

Remove the size from the heat, and strain it through cheesecloth or muslin into a bowl containing 1 litre (2 pt) of cold water.

If you will not be using all of the size at once, add 45 g (1½ oz) of moss size preservative, to prevent it turning sour. Stir it in thoroughly, and let the mixture stand for twelve hours, or overnight. This jelly needs to be kept at room temperature.

Preparation of colours

Special marbling colours are available, but poster paints can also be used.

Oxgall, a dispersing agent that makes colours flow evenly on the paper's surface, must be added to the paints. It is available at most good art shops.

All of the colours you have chosen should be mixed with oxgall in the proportion: 2 dessertspoons of colour to 1 teaspoon of oxgall. If any of the colours seem too thick and pasty, add more water. A single-cream consistency, falling freely from the end of a paintbrush, is about right.

Testing

A delicate balance between the size and the colour is needed for success with this technique. If the scales tip too far on either side, the whole effect will be ruined. It is best always to test the size mixture with one or two colours.

Fill the tray with the size in liquid form at room temperature: 3–5 cm (1½–2 in) in depth will be adequate.

Drop a spot of colour onto the size using a paintbrush. It should lie on the surface and expand in a circle to two or three times its original size. If it stays tight and static, add ¼ teaspoon more oxgall to the mixed colour. Then remove the first spot of colour with a newspaper skimmed over the surface and try again. If the colour still does not expand, the size is too thick and needs a little more water added to it. If the colour spreads too far, too much oxgall has been mixed with the colour, and more paint will have to be added. If the size is too

Moss marbling.

tray at least 63 × 45 cm (25 × 18 in)
   plastic or metal
125 g (4 oz) carragheen moss
125 g (4 oz) moss size preservative
prepared marbling colours (see pages
   124–25) or poster paint
oxgall
fine artists' paintbrushes
cocktail sticks
jam jars for mixing colours
cheesecloth, gauze or old stocking
saucepan
allum mordant

cold, this can sometimes cause the colour to spread. The colour may even sink to the bottom of the tray. A little warm water will soon cure this.

When you have tested one or two colours, try putting a drop of one on top of the other. You will see that the second stays unchanged. It is therefore necessary, if applying colour in this way, to add more oxgall to the second colour than to the first.

Preparation of paper (or fabric)

The paper must be treated with allum crystals dissolved in water before it is laid in the marbling tray.

Add 45 g (1½ oz) allum to 500 ml (1 pt) of hot water. Stir the crystals until they are dissolved and leave to cool.

A household sponge is used to apply the solution to the paper. A fine damping down is better than a soaking; if kept sandwiched between a sheet of glass and a heavy rubber matt, the paper should stay damp for a good three or four hours. This means that several sheets of paper can be prepared for a marbling session.

Method

If you can, have your tray conveniently placed near a running water supply. This will make the process easier, as water is used to wash off excess size from the paper as it is removed from the tray.

Skim lightly over the surface of the size with a newspaper to prevent particles in the atmosphere causing blemishes as the paint is worked on the surface.

Using a different brush for each colour, drop little spots of colour over the size covering an area 2–4 cm (1–2 in) larger than your sheet of paper. Leave enough room between each spot for the colours to expand, and enough space in between the colours for the different shapes of the design to be pulled out.

Cocktail sticks or the ends of fine paintbrushes make ideal tools for working the colours into the designed marble form. To begin with, it is best to work with just two colours. The patterning should be done as quickly as possible, being firm but gentle when coaxing the shapes into place.

Lay the damp paper in the tray letting it dip from the centre and then lowering it in evenly on both sides. This should prevent air bubbles getting trapped underneath it and ruining the effect. The paper is lifted out by taking hold of one side with the thumb and forefinger of both hands and lifting gently upwards. Hold the sheet of paper over the tray to let any excess size run off. Take it to the sink and place on the drainer. Fill a glass of water and gently pour it over the surface of the paper to remove all traces of size.

Skim over the surface of the size with newspaper to clean it before dropping in the colour for the next piece of paper.

Paper should be laid flat to dry in an even room temperature. If the paper buckles, iron it when completely dry with a moderate iron.

Alternative ideas

Breccia marble Stone-like blobs of colour, rather than swirling arabesque shapes, are made by dropping the first colour onto the surface in irregular-sized dots. Following the first colour, a second diluted with a little more oxgall is then flicked or dropped onto the size by hitting the brush against the side of a stick, causing the paint

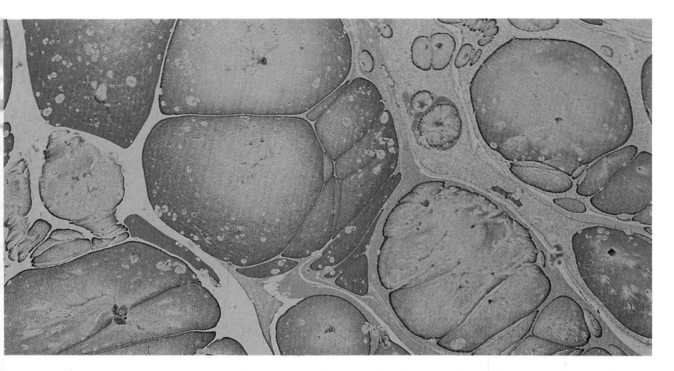

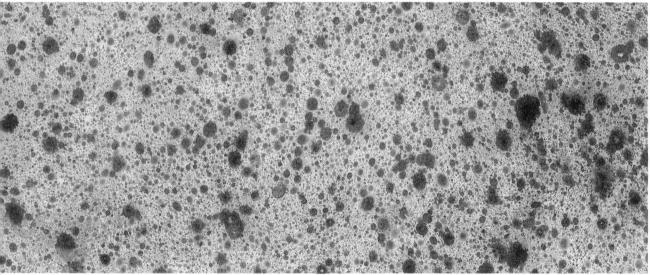

to scatter at random. A third colour, previously diluted with oxgall and a little water, can be applied. This last coat will expand at a greater rate than the first two, moving them into the desired stone-like blocks.

Granite and porphyry A diffuser can be used to great advantage in simulating this stone. It blows the finest speckles of paint onto the size. Two or three shades of the same colour with one contrasting colour or black and white, work beautifully.

Combing A traditional marble effect that has been produced in Italy for centuries. You can make a comb by pressing fine pins through a 1 × 1 cm (½ × ½ in) piece of balsa-wood which is then sandwiched between two pieces of cardboard and sealed for water-tightness with a polyurethane varnish (fig. 14). Made this way, it will last a very long time. The comb should be the same width as that of the tray you are using.

Top: *Breccia marble.*
Above: *Granite (with a diffuser).*

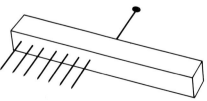

14 *Long, steel dress-making pins pushed through balsa-wood make an ideal comb.*

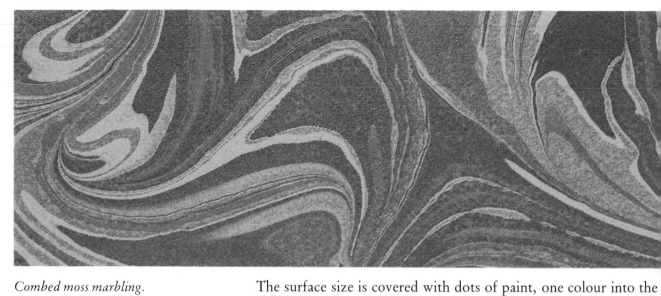

Combed moss marbling.

The surface size is covered with dots of paint, one colour into the middle of another, until you have rows of bull's eyes.

A cocktail stick or paintbrush tip is then drawn first through the bull's eyes in one direction, and then in the opposite direction to produce zig-zag stripes.

Take the comb with both hands and draw it through the zig-zags, the full length of the tray.

The effect should resemble the movement of electronically-controlled graphs: staccato waves of colour against colour.

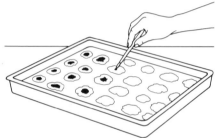

15.1 *Bull's-eye spots of colour are created by the addition of oxgall.*

15.2 *Use a cocktail stick, and then a comb, to draw the spots into one another to produce the traditional marble effect.*

9 SPECIAL MARBLE EFFECTS

The marble effects described in this chapter – lapis lazuli and malachite – are variations on the four marbling methods described in the previous chapter. You should refer to Chapter 1 for advice on the preparation of surfaces, apart from paper, and to Chapter 8 for general information on these methods.

LAPIS LAZULI

The beautiful blue of this mineral has rightly won it the name of heaven stone. Rare and expensive, it is not difficult to imagine how extravagant the ballroom of Catherine the Great of Russia looked when covered with it. However, it was not solely reserved for walls. A vase belonging to Francesco de Medici in the Pitti Palace, Florence, testifies to the wonderful qualities of this stone, and to the skill of the stone-carver who produced winged figures for handles in high relief, with icanthus leaves in low relief delicately balanced at the base.

Artists have used lapis lazuli, ground to a powder pigment, for painting in both oil and watercolours. Unfortunately, the price now

Part of a door and its surround: the pigments used for the blue marbling were vivid ultramarine on a base coat of grey blue with a touch of lavender. The green malachite effect was worked completely in water-based paint (gouache and poster colour mixed together): viridian and permanent green deep. A small amount of washing-up liquid acted as the catalyst to hold the water paint to the surface, whilst the veined strata was created by the resist action of methylated spirits.

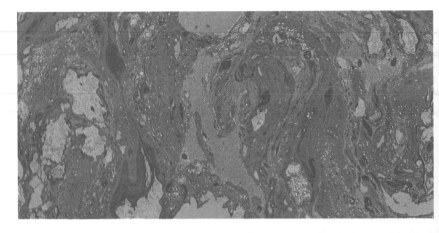

Lapis lazuli: controlled effect.

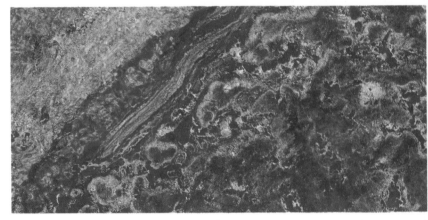

Lapis lazuli: fantasy effect.

makes it too costly, and a substitute ultramarine blue has taken its place on the artist's palette.

Chile and Afghanistan are two of the countries left with supplies, but the colour is nowhere near as deep as that of the Iranian or Russian stone. A grey figuring softens the overall blue colour and the flecks of gold, which look so distinctive in the deep blue of past pieces, are less outstanding, if indeed there are any there at all.

Oil glaze technique
(See pages 70–72)
Base colour: pale blue-grey
Prepare the glazes of ultramarine blue and Prussian blue in separate jars, each to a milky consistency.

Cover the surface with the ultramarine glaze.

Sponge this over to take away any lines that the paintbrush has left.

Add patches of Prussian blue with a brush to the glazed and sponged surface. These should cover about one-sixth of the area being worked. Sponge these patches to blend them in, but avoid making the colour too even.

Take a page of newspaper, squeeze it into a loose ball, and use it to remove areas of glaze. A pressing, rather than patting, movement should leave faceted lines on the glaze. Leave for five minutes.

Using two or three different-width artists' brushes loaded with white spirits, work a structure of veins across the glaze to expose the background grey.

Add a small amount of bronze powder to the white spirits. Take another, finer brush, load it with this mixture and, in nervous lines,

ultramarine, Prussian blue and white
  artists' oil paint
scumble glaze or home-made glazing
  liquid (see page 12)
white spirits
jars to mix colours in
bronze powder (gold)
soft cloth
newspaper
natural sponge
two 5 cm (2 in) household
  paintbrushes
paper towels

edge small areas of the darkest blue glaze. The white spirit should eat away at the glaze, leaving deposits of bronze powder as small cloud-like blemishes.

Leave this to dry completely, then seal with semi-matt or matt varnish. Avoid honey-coloured varnish as this can turn the blue to green with age.

Watercolour on an oil base (resist solvent method)
(See page 77)

Bronze powder is added either to the mixed gouache paints, if you want to create a lapis fantasy; or it is mixed with methylated spirits and added after the first application of methylated spirits, for a lighter, more controlled effect.

Base colour: pale blue-grey.

Mix the three gouache colours together in a jar or pot with enough water to make an opaque liquid. If this turns out to be transparent, add more paint, otherwise the lapis will look poor in depth. Add two or three drops of washing-up liquid to act as a catalyst.

If you want to create the more extravagant lapis look, mix a small quantity of bronze powder to the mixed paints. When the methylated spirits is applied, it will cause the bronze powder to separate out.

Cover the surface with the mixed gouache paint, working quickly and evenly with a 5 cm (2 in) paintbrush. It is important that this coat does not dry before you have finished the whole process.

With a 2 cm (1 in) hog's hair brush dipped in methylated spirits, run nervous lines through the paint, leaving an effect similar to the blue veins on a stilton cheese. Work quickly, as a dry spot anywhere on the surface could spoil the finish. Use the smaller artists' brushes for lifting out fine veins.

If you are creating the more reserved lapis effect, mix a little bronze powder with the methylated spirits. Paint it on just after the previous spirit application but before the paint has dried. Speed is crucial to success.

An interesting extra effect can be created by dipping a stencil brush into the bronze powder and methylated spirits mixture and flicking it gently with the forefinger over areas of the wet paint. This gives depth and authenticity to the marble look.

Wait until the surface is dry, and apply a semi-matt or matt varnish.

ultramarine, indigo, and Indian red gouache paint, mixed in the proportions: 2 parts ultramarine, 1 part indigo, ½ part Indian red
washing-up liquid
5 cm (2 in) brush
bronze powder
methylated spirits
pots for mixing colour in
selection of artists' brushes, including: 1 cm (½ in) soft hair, 5 mm (¼ in) soft hair, stencil brush

Alternative ideas
Mask off sections of the surface and work them individually to make it look as if the lapis has been layed in slabs. Alternatively, section off parts of the surface or object and cover these with contrasting marble to simulate inlay.

Oil colour on a water base
(See page 79)

For those who crave the grandeur of the past, sheets of marbled paper covering the walls and varnished over can transform the plainest of rooms into the palatial.

Paper: mid blue-grey; thin and slightly absorbent.

Mix the artists' oil colours in separate pots with white spirits to a single-cream consistency.

Using 60 ml (2½ fl oz) of size to every 1 litre (2 pt) of warm water,

indigo, ultramarine and Prussian blue artists' oil colour, mixed in separate pots with white spirits
rabbit-skin size or gelatine size (see page 79)
water
tray
fine artists' brushes
gold powder
white spirits
kitchen roll or newspaper
cocktail sticks

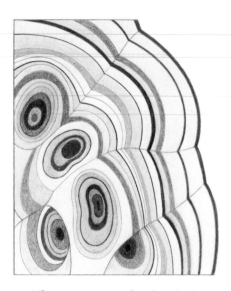

16 *The composition of real malachite. A study of the bull's-eye and strata formation will help the student to translate the quality of malachite into paintwork.*

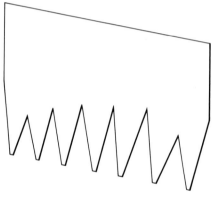

17 *Pointed teeth are fragile and do not leave their mark when being pulled through a glaze. Therefore make sure the teeth of your comb are cut flat, at least 2 mm (⅛ in) wide.*

viridian, phthalo green deep, and
   black artists' oil colour
scumble glaze or home-made glazing
   liquid (see page 12)
selection of artists' brushes (ox hair
   prefered)
white spirits
paper towels
jars for mixing paint in
thick cardboard for comb
scissors
2, 5 and 6 cm (1, 2 and 3 in) household
   paintbrushes

fill the tray to a depth of 1 cm (½ in).

Test the consistency of the size by dropping in a spot of one colour. It should expand to twice its original size. Refer to page 79 if problems arise.

Using a different brush for each colour, load each brush and cover the surface of the size with dots of paint.

Using cocktail sticks or the ends of your brushes, gently manoeuvre the colours into one another.

Using a fine brush, gently float the gold powder over parts of the surface. Irregular twists of the stick or brush will help disperse it amongst the oil.

When you are satisfied with the designed marble, take a sheet of paper, holding it with both hands so the centre is inclined towards the size and oil colour. Let it down quickly but gently into the tray.

Lift up the paper using the thumb and forefinger of both hands, and let the excess size drip off the paper over the tray.

Lay the paper on newspaper and leave it to dry. If it buckles, iron it with an ordinary domestic iron.

To apply this to a wall, use a ready-mix, strong, wallpaper paste. Seal the surface with an emulsion glaze on completion. Varnish with a semi-matt or gloss varnish, as preferred.

MALACHITE

Looking at first glance like a wonderful lush green map of the ocean floor, malachite is one of the most distinctive and beautiful of all minerals. It ranges in colour from aquamarine, through turquoise, to apple green and emerald; in shade, from bottle green to black.

Fantasy after fantasy can easily be created because the patterning of malachite is infinitely different within each piece. The overall impression is of bands of colours, ringed in some instances like bull's eyes seen through a distorting mirror. Sharp angles appear to break the continuous flow as one bulky knuckle, ringed and outlined, meets the next. The consolidated whole is a marvellous example of nature's artistry.

Malachite has been simulated by many decorative artists in the past on both furniture and objects, combs of cardboard being used to space the bands of colour. Brushes can be used for working a free, flowing movement giving an individual fantasy to the piece, but the process is slowed down considerably and should be kept for small areas of decorative art work.

Oil glaze technique
(See pages 70–72)
Base colour: aquamarine or leaf green (blue green rather than yellow green).
Mix the oil colours in separate pots wth enough scumble glaze and white spirits, or home-made glaze, to give a thin, creamy liquid. The colour should be strong rather than completely transparent. Test a small area before proceeding.

Cut a strip of cardboard 6 × 10 cm (3 × 4 in). Make irregular V-shaped cuts on one of the shorter sides to create a row of teeth. Make sure the edges are perfectly clean and straight (fig. 17).

Take the largest household paintbrush and cover the whole piece with viridian glaze.

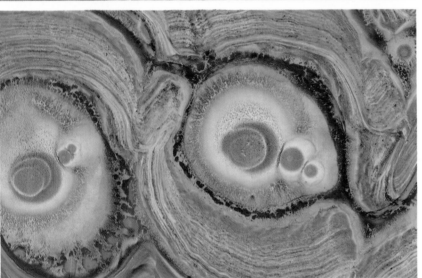

Left *Malachite: oil glaze.*
Below left *Malachite: watercolour on an oil base.*

1

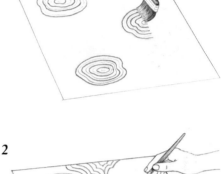

2

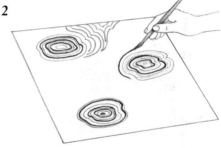

3

Using the same brush, in a twisting movement, rotate rings of phthalo green as random circles over 20 per cent of the surface (fig. 18.1).

Dip the 2 cm (1 in) brush into the black glaze and outline some of the circles. In other parts, centre the brush and twist without moving it about, then lift it off (fig. 18.2).

With the ox hair brushes dipped into phthalo green, cover the spaces in between these circles, undulating around them in a continuous flow. The brush can be reversed sharply in some places to give an angular break to the glaze (fig. 18.3).

Using the comb, work into some of the circles with a bold, circular motion, using zig-zag jerky movements if possible on some of the outside edges of the circles. You will find with practice how to use the comb as an extension of the eye, and control over these patterns will come naturally (fig. 18.4).

When satisfied with your malachite, leave it to dry completely. Then seal it with two coats of semi-matt varnish.

The base colour can be changed if a deeper look is needed. Using a blue-black base coat and working from a dark green glaze, build up rings and eyes all the way through to light aquamarine. The difference in look is quite extraordinary.

4

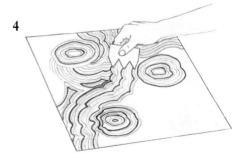

18 *Malachite: oil glaze method.*

19 Malachite veneer as a border on a table-top can look very original.

Alternative ideas

Brush malachite Using artists' brushes of different widths and quality, coat the whole surface with phthalo green glaze and work bands and circles with viridian and all shades mixed through to black. As a guide, fig. 16 illustrates the formation of malachite, which you should follow in your own colour bands.

Malachite veneer Malachite is often seen this way on table-tops and decorative bases for statuary and candelabra. Thin slithers are cut from the same piece and are put together to create repeated patterns and shapes. Flower-heads with multi-veined petals look quite acceptable when executed as a table-top in malachite.

This effect is achieved in paintwork by masking off sections, or by pencilling in the sections, and working on them one at a time. Combs and brushes can both be used.

Watercolour on an oil base (resist solvent method)
(See page 77)

This method is very simple. The secret of success is speed. The best results are obtained by working on a horizontal rather than vertical plane.

Base colour: pale blue-green.

Mix each of the gouache paints in a separate container with enough water to give a thin, single-cream consistency. A drop of washing-up liquid will act as a catalyst to bind the paint to the surface.

Using the 5 cm (2 in) paintbrush dipped into the viridian pot, cover the area being marbled with undulating lines, broken by occasional circles (fig. 20.1).

Using the 2 cm (1 in) hog's hair brushes with oxide of chromium and, in moderation the black paint, outline and follow the circles of viridian. This application must be done quickly before any paint begins to dry out (fig. 20.2).

Load the third hog's hair brush with methylated spirits and pull it through the paint following the flow of real malachite (fig. 20.3).

Bands of separating colour should show the base coat as well as fusing together the colours which were applied separately.

The stencil brush filled with methylated spirits can be flicked over small areas of the work, but be careful in doing this as a paint build-up on the surface can take a long time to dry out and cause untidy

designer's gouache paint: viridian, oxide of chromium and small amount of black
three 2 cm (1 in) wide hog's hair brushes
methylated spirits
stencil brush
jars for mixing paint in
5 cm (2 in) soft bristle brush
water and washing-up liquid

1 **2** **3**

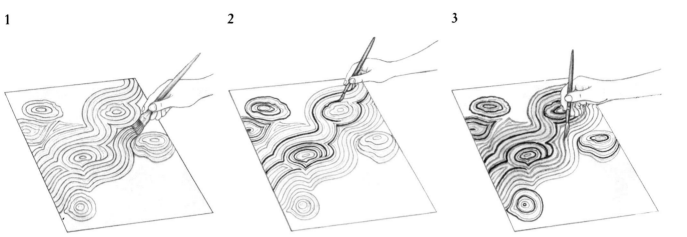

20 *Malachite: watercolour on an oil base.*

blobs of colour that spoil the precise flow of the real malachite.

Leave the work to dry out naturally. Seal with two coats of semi-matt or gloss varnish, as preferred.

Alternative ideas

For a small object that can be easy layed with metallic foil, try experiments with this technique in shades of honey, brown and umber. The result is a tiger's eye stone appearance. It does not have to be a known mineral as far as the colours are concerned. A fantasy look can be sensational if created in blues or dark reds over an appropriate base colour.

Oil colour on a water base
(See page 79)
Back to the marbling tray for this translation of malachite.
Paper: blue-green; fine, slightly absorbent.
Fill the tray to a depth of approximately 2 cm (1 in) with size.

Mix oil colours in separate pots with white spirits to a single-cream consistency.

Test one of the colours on the size first by taking a fine brush, load it with paint and put a drop onto the size. It should grow to twice its original size. Refer to page 79 if problems arise.

Aim for large spots of colour to begin with. The pressure of these rings one against the other is needed to simulate the stone.

When you have covered an area bigger than your paper with these large circles of paint, pull out thin bands from the circles to create spiralling bands around some of the spots. Be as light-handed as possible with this. It should look like a gentle flow and not a tidal wave of movement.

When satisfied with the surface, take the paper in both hands. Holding it in position above the tray, let the centre of the paper down onto the water and release it from your hands. This should prevent air bubbles being trapped underneath the paper.

Take hold of the paper with the forefinger and thumb of both hands, lift it up and hold it over the tray until the excess size has drained away.

Let the paper dry on newspaper, at room teperature. Iron it when dry if necessary, to flatten it out.

marbling tray 63 × 45 cm (25 × 18 in)
rabbit-skin granules, or gelatine (see page 79)
phthalo green, viridian and black artists' oil colours
white spirits
paper towels
fine artists' brushes
cocktail sticks
newspaper
jars for mixing colours

Moss marbling
(See pages 80–82)

For the most realistic of all malachite interpretations, this technique is unsurpassed. It provides such tight control over the suspended paint that you can duplicate the flow of the stone to a minute fraction.

It is very important that the size and the paint are mixed to the right consistency, and that the colour is correct. The paint can be viridian in various shades to almost black, or turquoise green and viridian mixed with black, to give four or five different shades.

Paper: very pale blue-green.

Prepare the Carragheen moss size the night before you want to use it. Remember to add the preservative if you wish to keep it for more than one or two days.

Fill the tray with enough size to give a depth of 2 cm (1 in).

Mix the shades of green in separate pots, testing the difference between each on a scrap of white paper. Three or four different shades should be enough for your first attempts. The overall effect of these shades can be altered by the addition of oxgall and water after the first applications. This will reduce the surface tension of the paint, allowing it to spread on the size. It also has to be used if you are dropping on colour, otherwise the paint will not spread.

Test one or two spots of colour on the surface. Refer to pages 81–82 if problems arise.

Clear the size by skimming a newspaper over the surface.

With brushes or cocktail sticks loaded with paint, cover the surface of the size with spots. Try to keep them touching one another as this distortion from the circular into an irregular kidney shape has a more realistic look.

For the next application, add a little more water and a drop of oxgall to the mixed paints. Drop this shade on alternating shade with shade until you have covered the size surface once more.

Repeat the whole procedure again with another addition of water and oxgall. Be careful not to overdo it, as the circles produced in this last application should be smaller than the first ones. Test one area if you are not sure, and then dilute the paints accordingly.

When satisfied with the green pebble effect, take a cocktail stick and work into the circles of colour, splitting some completely in half, making indented petal shapes on others, and pulling bands over other circles in an arabesque design.

When satisfied, take the paper and dampen it down with a sponge soaked in allum mordant (see page 82). Leave it for a minute, then pick up by both hands, lower it centre first onto the size and let it rest on the surface colour.

Pick up the paper with the forefinger and thumb of both hands and let it drip over the tray for a few seconds. Transfer it to the sink and sluice down gently with cold water from a jug.

Leave it to dry on newspaper at room temperature. If it has buckled, a quick iron, when it is completely dry, will flatten it down again.

marbling colours pre-mixed, or designer's poster gouache: viridian or turquoise, black
tray
Carragheen moss
moss size preservative
oxgall
allum mordant
cocktail sticks
brushes for mixing paint
pots or jars to hold paint
cheesecloth or muslin for straining size
newspaper

Opposite: A veritable pot pourri *of marbling techniques; table-tops, mirror-frames, clocks, pencil-holders, tissue-box covers and fans. Unfortunately, what the picture does not show are the bed-heads, the pianos and the car bonnets which would go further to show that any surface can become a marbled fantasy!*

10 TORTOISE-SHELL

Owing to the establishment of the Silk Route, the Chinese influence penetrated many aspects of European life, and it is quite likely that the materials and methods of decorative shell inlay were brought to Europe along with the silks and spices.

By the sixteenth century, Italian artisans had developed a technique of inlaying tortoise-shell with pewter into a solid ground. And by the beginning of the seventeenth century, craftsmen in France, Holland and Germany had begun to manufacture furniture and *objets d'art* using the same method.

The peak of perfection for all tortoise-shell veneer work rests in France on the work-benches of a court cabinet-maker named André Charles Boulle. Unfortunately, the name Boulle is now given to all tortoise-shell and metal inlay work, irrelevant of when or where it was manufactured. Considering that resin, plastic and wax have all since been used to duplicate the qualities of this decorative shell, Mr Boulle must surely be turning in his cabinet.

21 *A gradual softening and blending of shapes and colours make tortoise-shell one of the most pleasing of all decorative surface finishes.*

A painted finish using oil colour and varnish was practised in England and America along with chinoiserie and lacquerwork. Examples of painted tortoise-shell dating to the seventeenth century still exist.

Three different techniques are described in this chapter that all create the luxurious depth and appeal of tortoise-shell.

FRENCH ENAMEL VARNISH

This thin varnish comes in a great variety of colours. It is easy to brush onto any non-absorbent surface, has a very fast drying time and is transparent. For this tortoise-shell technique, the varnish needs to be applied very quickly as does the solvent used to break the surface tension thus creating the uneven depth of colour exhibited in the real shell.

Surface preparation: Any kind of non-absorbent surface is suitable; the base colour for this natural tortoise-shell should be a strong creamy yellow. Two coats of mid-sheen, oil-based paint or quick car-spray cellulose will do admirably.

Work on a horizonatal surface only.

Put three or four tablespoons of each varnish colour into containers or jars that allow you to dip brushes in and out with speed.

Using the yellow varnish on a wide paintbrush, cover the whole area that you intend to tortoise-shell in random blotches. It will spread readily. Don't worry too much as the next two applications, of raw umber and red-brown, should do the same, giving the piece or panel a dappled quality (fig. 22.1).

Saving the black for the last application, put small spots onto the still-wet varnish in radiating diagonals that become heavier towards one corner (fig. 22.2 & 3).

Fill the household brush with methylated spirits, take the length of wood with one hand and tap the brush against its edge over the surface varnish (fig. 22.4).

The instant the methylated spirits hits the wet varnish, it starts to eat its way in, dispersing the varnish in some cases to a diameter three or four times greater than the original drop of spirit.

French enamel varnish: raw umber, mid-yellow, red-brown and black
jars for holding varnish colour
4 soft-bristled artists' brushes
paper towels
5 cm (2 in) household paintbrush
30 cm (12 in) length of wood
methylated spirits

22 *Tortoise-shell: French enamel varnish method.*

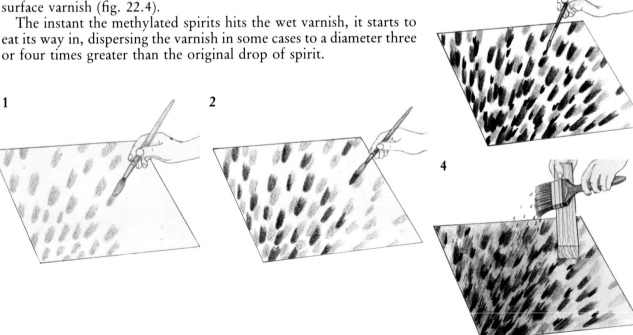

Leave the varnish to dry completely before sealing it with a polyurethane varnish. Methylated-spirit-based varnishes should be avoided as they could lift the surface.

Alternative ideas

Change the base coat to scarlet or vermillion and use only raw sienna, burnt umber and black varnish.

Change the base coat to a yellow green and use raw sienna, burnt umber and black.

For vertical surfaces, attempt no more than 0.10 sq m (1 sq ft) at a time and be prepared for the varnish and methylated spirits to run. This can look very attractive, but you must know how far you can take this before it goes out of control and starts to look messy.

There are metallic foil wallpapers for sale in gold and silver that can be given this effect. It is best to have two people working on these, one applying the varnish, the other the spirit.

OIL PAINT ON AN OIL BASE WITH VARNISH

Small pieces of real tortoise-shell can still be picked up inexpensively. Bric-a-brac and charity shops are the places to start your search, looking out for items such as hairbrush mounts, ornamental combs, pill-box lids and gaming counters, you will find it helpful to study a piece before starting work in this method. Maximum effect is achieved on a small area. An area larger than 50 sq cm (18 sq in) will pose problems with the directional streaking and look monotonous. And the piece would be likely to overpower anything else of decorative value in the room.

Surface preparation: Any non-porous surface can be worked on, even laminate, but do test a small section before you start. If the paint sinks in, seal the surface with a coat of quick-drying varnish before starting work.

The base colour can be either yellow, for a natural tortoise-shell effect, red or green. It is very important to mix the base colour correctly. A red that is too brown or blue will kill the feeling of depth and transparency. Likewise, a yellow that veers towards cream will result in a washed-out tortoise-shell.

Mix in a jar enough varnish with white spirits, in a ratio of 60 per cent varnish to 40 per cent spirits, to cover twice the total area to be worked.

Take one half the mixture and divide it among four containers.

Add one colour to each (raw sienna, raw umber, burnt umber and black). Brush stir thoroughly until the oil colour has dispersed.

For natural tortoise-shell only, take a little yellow ochre and add this to the other half of the varnish and spirits mixture. Stir until you have a thin golden wash of varnish and spirit.

Using a varnishing or similar brush, apply the varnish and spirits wash to the total surface area quickly. (For red and green Boulle, the mix is applied without colour.)

Take a paper towel and blot over the surface. This will create a dappled look and at the same time remove excess varnish.

Using the raw sienna varnish mixture and a 1 cm (½ in) artists' brush, work streaks in a disjointed diagonal across the piece (fig. 23.1).

Yellow base (buttery): Cadmium mid to deep yellow with a small amount of white.
Red base (bright pillar-box): Scarlet and vermillion will both work well as the base colour.
Green base (apple green): Oxide of chromium or terre verte (one-third yellow and two-thirds white, mixed)
polyurethane gloss varnish
artists' oil colours: raw sienna, raw umber, burnt umber and black; and yellow ochre for natural tortoise-shell
white spirits
selection of artists' brushes (soft hair with points)
5 cm (2 in) varnishing brush
pots or jars for mixing paint
paper towels

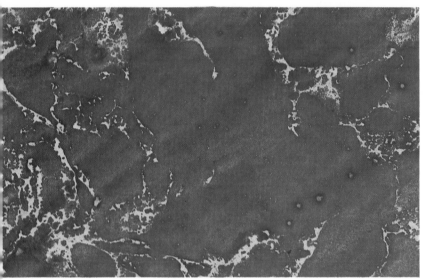

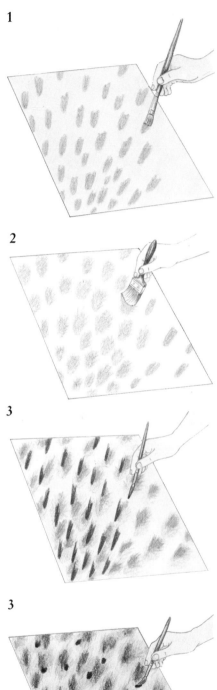

Left *Tortoise-shell: oil colour and varnish.*
Below left *Tortoise-shell: oil on a water base.*

1

2

3

3

Using the varnish (or similar) brush, wiped on a paper towel, lightly brush over the raw sienna streaks (fig. 23.2).

The burnt sienna varnish is treated in the same way, but it should be applied with a fine brush and the streaks should be smaller. Work in the same direction over the top of the raw sienna. The real shell has denser streaks of smaller proportions fanning out from an imaginary central point. Brush over the streaks with the varnish brush.

The raw umber varnish is applied with a still smaller brush, in streaks, which should be blended in, working in both directions (fig. 23.3).

Next, apply small irregular dots, rather than streaks, of black varnish over the surface. These should be kept to a minimum and cover no more than half the radius of the tortoise-shell fan, becoming slightly more dense towards one corner (fig. 23.4). Brush gently in both directions to blend in the black dots.

Leave to dry out completely.

Cover with coat of the varnish mixture tinted with yellow ochre if you still have some left. Alternatively, use full-strength polyurethane semi-matt varnish.

23 *Tortoise-shell: oil on an oil base.*

Natural tortoise-shell effect using an oil paint on an oil base with varnish has transformed a mirror-frame that had been thrown out by its owner. The base coat was a bright yellow, mid-sheen paint; followed by raw sienna, raw umber, burnt umber and black oil colour in varnish.

Alternative ideas

Use the same colours and method over Dutch metal or aluminium foil.

Mask off areas and use a contrast technique on them. Ebony or ivory teamed with tortoise-shell looks very elegant.

Stencil over the tortoise-shell with poor man's gold (see page 50) to simulate brass or pewter inlay.

WATER ON AN OIL BASE (REVERSE TECHNIQUE)

Brush and splatter work are combined in this fantasy tortoise-shell effect, and a little thought and preparation may help this easy method to succeed well enough to fool the many rather than the few. Consider where the radiating brush strokes should go, and what the effect of the methylated spirits will be as it breaks the tension of the paint. Try out the technique on sample boards or glossy card first (such as Kromekote, see pages 124–25).

Surface preparation: oil-based paint in yellow, red or green (see page 96).

designer's gouache: raw umber and black
methylated spirits
containers for paints and spirits
selection of artists' brushes
polyurethane or acrylic varnish
water and paper towels
washing-up liquid

Mix each of the gouache colours in separate containers with water to a milky consistency, adding a drop of washing-up liquid as a catalyst.

Keep the methylated spirits at hand in a jar beside the work.

With a 1–2 cm (½ in) brush, cover 50 to 60 per cent of the base coat with streaks of raw umber approximately 1–5 cm (½–2 in) long, radiating outwards and upwards along a diagonal line (fig. 24.1).

Take a smaller brush and apply the black gouache and water mix to the tips of these streaks (fig. 24.2).

Take two brushes of different widths and dip them into the methylated spirits. Then run them over the gouache streaks, working on the same diagonal. The colours should begin to merge together and at the same time the streaks should separate to show the base coat. A fine, clean brush dipped into the spirits can be used to emphasize the directional flow if the colours merge together too much (fig. 24.3).

For a transparent quality, soak a paper towel in methylated spirits and blot some of the denser areas of colour towards the outside edges.

Leave this to dry completely. Seal with a semi-matt varnish.

ALTERNATIVE IDEAS FOR TORTOISE-SHELL

If you make sample cards, don't throw them away. Cut them into 5 cm (2 in) squares and use them with squares of black card to make a sensational chess board.

Strips 1–2 cm (½–1 in) wide look particularly stylish set into the recesses of picture and mirror frames.

Mask off areas on a large surface and create patterns and designs with pieces of tortoise-shell card in the same way as real shell is used. This treatment works well on small, circular table-tops and trays.

1

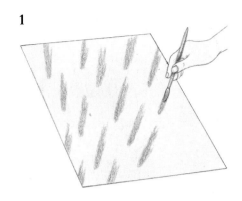

2

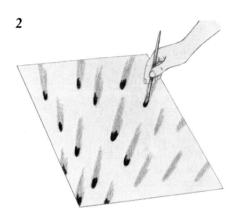

3

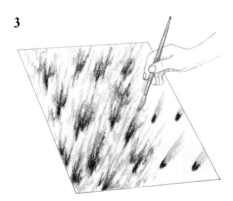

24 *Tortoise-shell: watercolour on an oil base.*

11 *BAMBOOING*

It is difficult to understand, when looking into the garden-shed at the bamboo canes purchased for pennies, just why the public went crazy for the first pieces of Chinese bamboo furniture that were imported into Europe back in the eighteenth century. Demand soon outstripped supply, owing to the length of the journey from the East, and European craftsmen, taking full advantage of the slow boats to China, started to turn out their own versions of bamboo furniture to keep the busy market appeased. Since that time, bamboo furniture, both real and imitation, has been given many new leases of life.

In Europe, the bamboo boom occurred in the 1920s and 1930s. Unfortunately, these pieces are turning up in antique and junk shops in very poor condition. To the rescue then! With the kindly assistance of your brush and paints, give another breath of life to the hedgerow of the Orient.

Surface preparation for real bamboo

Make sure the surface is completely stripped of varnish and oil. A cloth soaked in methylated spirits and rubbed over it two or three times, will remove oil and light varnish.

If the bamboo has already been painted, wire wool should be used over the entire piece to key in the coats of paint: two coats of mid-sheen, oil-based paint is the ideal base for any decorative paintwork. The colour is entirely up to you.

Surface preparation for imitation bamboo (European turned wood)

If painted, strip back to the surface with a normal paint-stripper. It is a long process, but it sharpens up the knuckle-like rings in the wood.

Apply a reasonably thin coat of undercoat to this surface and sand down lightly.

Follow with two coats of mid-sheen, oil-based paint, lightly sanding down after the first coat. This will give the piece a really smooth finish.

If you have no time to strip old paintwork, sand down or rub over with wire wool to key in the two coats of paint.

DECORATIVE PAINTWORK

Method 1 – high-relief colour

This positive way of painting bamboo gives the boldest of all decorative finishes. By emphasizing nature's own work on the rings and knots inherent in bamboo, you create in colour the depth and character of the piece.

Mix medium-depth shade of your chosen colour with either acrylic medium or white spirits, depending on which type of paint you are using. This colour must be transparent. If it is thick and opaque, the bamboo will look heavy and amateurish.

Using a flat 1 cm (½ in) wide artists' brush, paint this thin wash over the ring knuckles of the wood (fig. 25.1). If the wash drips, run

acrylic paints or model-makers' enamels (artists' oil paint will take too long to dry and may smudge)
fine artists' paintbrushes
2 cm (1 in) paintbrush or lacquer brush
pots for mixing colours
paper towels
acrylic medium or white spirits

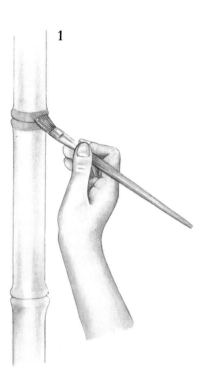

1

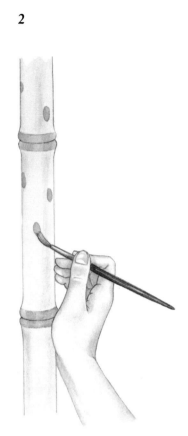

2

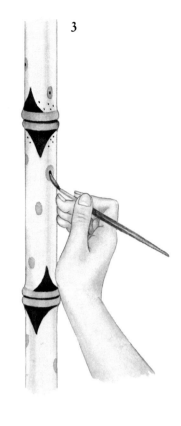

3

25.1 *Brush over knuckle growth joints with a contrast glaze colour.*
25.2 *Apply spots with a fine artists' brush.*
25.3 *Painted growth lines add character and form.*
25.4 *Extended growth lines and vertical stripes create a bamboo fantasy.*

4

the brush down the drip and blend it in with the overall base colour. A happy mistake like this can work very well.

Take a fine, pointed brush next and with the same colour wash, spot the paint at random intervals on part of the bamboo stem. These ovals should be no more than 5–10 mm (¼–½ in) in size (fig. 25.2).

Mix a darker shade of the colour you are using. Or alternatively, you could use a contrasting colour to the wash and background colour. Using a fine brush, paint in the growth spines that run up and down the bamboo stem from the knuckles.

Paint a fine band of the darker or contrasting colour around the middle of the knuckle joints. Then add dots and spots around, and in the middle of, the oval markings on the stem (fig. 25.3).

Finally add the extended points of the spine. Working with the finest brush, pull out elongated and slightly curved lines from the knuckles (fig. 25.4).

Wait for the paint to dry before sealing. This can be done with acrylic semi-matt varnish or polyurethane semi-matt varnish.

Method 2 – low-relief colour

The subtle look of pastels and soupy half-tones gives a quiet elegance to a large piece of bamboo furniture. This technique is very suitable for a decorative scheme that is highly colour co-ordinated.

Mix in three different pots with white spirits if using model enamel medium or water for acrylics, quantities of colour varying from a thin wash as the overall colour to a deeper-toned thicker paint and finally, the darkest tone of all.

Working with a 2 cm (1 in) brush and the light wash, cover the surface of the piece, dragging rather than brushing, with a thin coat of colour.

Wipe around the knuckle joints with a soft rag to remove the colour back to the base paint (fig. 26.1).

The medium tone of paint is now applied with a finer brush either side of the knuckle joints leaving the widest rings uncovered. These lines should be vertical rather than circular and blended into the wash (fig. 26.2).

26.1 *With a soft cloth, glaze is removed from the growth joints.*
26.2 *Shadows that highlight the knuckles above and below are applied with a soft artists' brush.*
26.3 *Elegance in both form and colour can be achieved with the use of fine vertical lines painted over the softened shadows.*

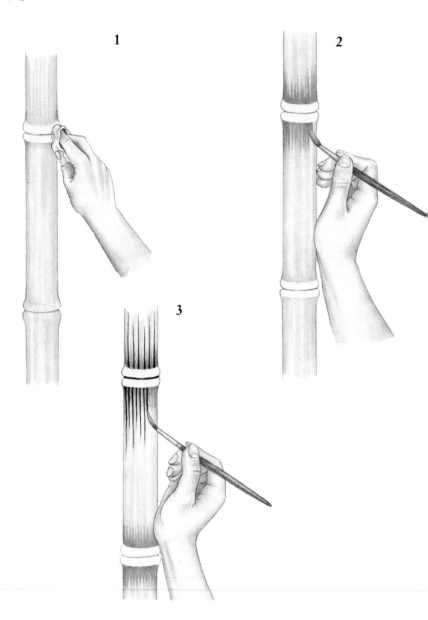

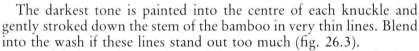

The sympathetic colourings of this Georgian faux bamboo chair gives away no idea of its original condition. It had been painted many times in its life and the only way to achieve a good surface on the chair again was to strip it down to bare wood and start from the beginning. Primer/sealer was followed by undercoat, followed by two coats of sandy beige. The glaze used for the main body work was a soft green gold, and the high relief knuckles were picked out in chestnut brown and dark grey.

The darkest tone is painted into the centre of each knuckle and gently stroked down the stem of the bamboo in very thin lines. Blend into the wash if these lines stand out too much (fig. 26.3).

Wait for the surface to dry and then seal. For an antique look, a light, oak wood-stain varnish can be applied; diluted with an equal amount of white spirits or methylated spirits, depending on the varnish base.

PAINTED BAMBOO EFFECT

A staircase in the Royal Pavilion, Brighton, although made of cast iron, has all the illusion of genuine bamboo. The realistic colours employed on its surface are beautifully deceptive.

To trick the eye into believing a moulding or flat surface is bamboo is not difficult. It can be done on tubular metal, and rounded mouldings in metal or wood. No more than one colour need be used and the method of application of paint once mastered can look totally convincing.

Surface preparation: see Chapter 1.

Mix the colour of your choice in three separate containers with white spirits or acrylic medium, depending on the type of paint used. The colours should be diluted with water or spirits into three strengths: light wash, medium wash and dark wash.

model enamel paints, or acrylics
selection of artists' brushes
paper towels
jars or pots for mixing colour

Start with the light wash and work all over the piece, moulding or cylinder with a dragged effect.

Taking the medium shade next, decide where the knuckles and joints are to be, brush a 1 cm (½ in) wide strip at each point, and blend in.

With the darkest colour, and this is the trick, paint a thin shadowy line in the centre of each band to give the appearance of depth, thereby creating pairs of knuckles.

With the same dark wash, dot and streak small areas above and below these knuckles and blend into the lightest wash.

Using the brush, wiped on a paper towel, create highlights on either side of the darkest wash lines.

Shade the sides of the moulding or cylinder to give the impression that the bamboo stem narrows near each joint, and shade under the joints as if caught by natural sunlight.

ALTERNATIVE IDEAS FOR BAMBOOING

Black lacquer with bands of gold around the knuckle joints goes far into the realms of chinoiserie fantasy.

Make your own stylized bamboo by gluing small plastic curtain-rings over a piece of 1 cm (½ in) dowelling. Painted with one of the techniques in this chapter, no one would guess that it was not a turned piece of wood.

27 *A piece of flat or curved moulding can take on all the character of bamboo with a little imagination and a spot of trompe l'oeil brushwork.*

12 TROMPE L'OEIL (TRICK-OF-THE-EYE)

The pure magic of decorative paintwork can be seen at its best in the illusionary painting technique known as 'trompe l'oeil'. A deception created with light, shade and perspective on a flat surface should, if it is to be successful, trick the eye of the beholder into believing it has all the volume and form of a third dimension.

Examples from the past range from gigantic vistas with architectural effects on a monumental scale, to filigree tracery as delicate as lace. The church painters of Renaissance Italy had a field day with domes sporting trailing vines, and foreshortened figures peering over balustrades while their pet monkeys delight in climbing over the masonry. A favourite device was that of angels peering through a sky filled with bun-shaped clouds. It takes very many years of study and practice to become proficient in the art of trick painting. It is necessary to have an artist's eye for colour composition, good imagination, and a great deal of time.

For those who want to try their hand at this often light-hearted interpretation of decorative work, the first requirement is an understanding of the subtlties of light and shadow. The second requirement is a good eye for copying. This is not cheating. Many an artist with great talent has copied another artist's work. In fact, if you consider most artist's paintings, they are only copying nature's artistry in their own style.

Do not fret about the quality or subject matter to start with. A simple object, such as a door handle, can work beautifully. Ribbons and bows painted on a wall, appearing to hold up a real picture-frame, is another idea. The points to remember for a really convincing finish are illustrated by the drawings in this chapter.

Always take into account the natural light source in the room. There may be more than one, in which case look at the objects or

The mixing of artists' colours is kept to a minimum in this beautifully conceived piece of trompe l'oeil painting. A simple Delft pottery wall-bracket and vase look ready to take a bunch of garden flowers.

28

29

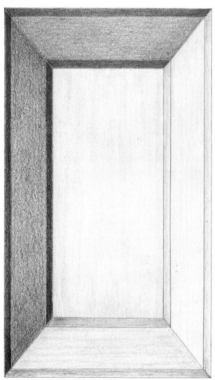

30

furniture around the area where the subject is to be painted. Study the highlights and shadows of the natural light.

Sketch your subject on a piece of tracing-paper and mark the highlights and shadows on it, checking them against other objects in that part of the room. The tracing-paper can be used later to transfer your design onto the wall.

If there is no direct light source and you have to create one, study the effects of the electric lighting in the room. Wall lights cast wonderfully strange shadows; up-lighting from table lamps can be very dramatic. Choose a light source that gives the most shade and light on the directional perspective of your subject. Trompe l'oeil painting at times only works if you are standing at one position in the room.

Balustrading, marble columns, decorative garden urns and door panelling give this corner of a London dining-room a touch of the Renaissance Palace.
28 *An exercise to test the eye and your artistry. As well as reproducing the highlights and shadows on the object itself, you must reproduce the shadow that would be cast by the object.*
29 *Trompe l'oeil panelling can give a surface many added dimensions.*
30 *A balustrade running round a room achieves a feeling of space beyond that can be treated to even more spectacular trompe l'oeil effects.*

There are no rules about the mediums or brushes to use in trick painting. Oil colours certainly enable an artist to move the colour around for longer periods of time, but this can lead to time being wasted, waiting for passages of paint to dry. Acrylic paints are good to start off with, and mediums that retard the drying time and flowing quality of the paint can be used. Thin acrylic washes create a transparent look, but do bear in mind that the colour you mix can dry considerably darker than it appears on the pallet. Test the colour first on a sample board if you are in doubt.

It is always advisable to draw the work on paper first. It does not have to be the exact size. Sketches to scale will give you a better idea of proportion if you know how to square them up or down when applying the design to the surface.

If you have made the drawing full-size, make a tracing and transfer this directly onto the wall or piece being painted. Lead pencil marks show through transparent glazes so do be careful when drawing in. Smudges and heavy pencilling will make the end result look grey and messy.

Work from dark paint to light paint as far as possible. If you have the time, under-painting the form of the subject will add greater depth.

The surface must be prepared correctly if the medium used is going to remain on the wall or object. For the most part when using oil or acrylic paints, a base coat of oil-based paint is required. Undercoat, if applied in two or three coats, will do admirably but usually needs tinting. Stainers or artists' oil colours will do this.

With water techniques, the addition of a catalyst such as washing-up liquid or fine plaster filler will keep the paint on an oil-based surface, but there is no reason why a porous, water-based finish should not be used. However, it will take speed and dexterity to handle this method of working, for drying is almost instant and mistakes have to be covered over before you can start again.

TROMPE L'OEIL MURALS

Your confidence will increase as you become used to working with this technique. And as your ideas become more ambitious, you could try tackling a larger area.

A simple, single motif can be repeated over and over again around a room and still be called trompe l'oeil. Again, the first consideration is light and shade in the context of the natural light source entering the room.

Panelling and dado rails are an easy subject for trompe l'oeil over a large area; colour, measurements and proportions are the elements to get right. A ruler, pencil, and long straight-edge are the basic requirements; a plumb-line can help if the walls look out of true.

Marbled panels combined with skirting-boards and cornice give a palatial grandeur to an entrance hall. Balustrading can add extra dimensions to a room, making it appear both longer and wider. For a

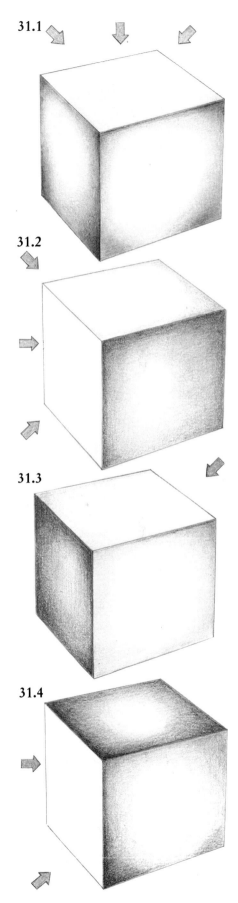

31.1

31.2

31.3

31.4

Study the effects of the light falling on the object you are painting.
31.1 *Light source from above and right-hand side.*
31.2 *Light source from the back and left-hand side.*
31.3 *Light source from the right, both above and below.*
31.4 *Light source from the side centrally and from below.*

Stencil work on library shelves, using a grey green acrylic paint in two colours, works as an exercise in trompe l'oeil shadowing. The simple motif creates an under-played, rather than exotic, effect.

touch of the country, why not try a garden fence. If you could team this up with the clouding technique described on pages 25–26 and add a sunflower or two, you will soon have the whole room coming together in trompe l'oeil.

The challenge of a large room involves a lot of preparatory work and many drawings need to be done before painting begins. However, if your design includes a repeated subject you can reduce the amount of time involved by using a stencil. A series of identical shapes can be accomplished in hours rather than days.

Another time-saver, and certainly something for the relative newcomer to large areas of decorative paintwork to consider, is to keep the colouring to a minimum. The traditional method known as grisaille painting uses only one colour plus black and white. It can work wonders if your choice of subject is architectural. In fact statuary, carved reliefs, and columns that lift a ceiling skywards, may appear over the top, or fail completely, if a lot of colour is used.

Trompe l'oeil painting has existed for thousands of years, and no doubt artists will be painting illusions on the moon if they are given half a chance. It bridges the gap between decorative painter and true artist; there is no dividing line. A butterfly painted on a wall for fun; an oil painting hanging in a museum: each has its own legitimate place, and both can give the same amount of pleasure.

13 DECORATING FURNITURE

How do you make the most out of that ghastly heap of old furniture tucked away in the attic or cellar: a fitting sub-title for this chapter perhaps? There surely must be something worth saving about the piece that nobody loves anymore; it should not be allowed to die on a dump or succumb to a skip.

The answer, of course, is to give it a new identity. This is not difficult, and need not be expensive. Brush it to freedom with a fresh coat of paint using a technique from one of the previous chapters, and you will soon change your mind about sending it to an early grave. Junk shops overflow with odds and ends of furniture that, for the price of a meal in a restaurant, can be transformed into an eye-catching, welcome addition to the home.

If you think your piece of furniture is of good quality, but that it is horridly unattractive, get a second opinion on its value before beginning work on it. It could turn out to be worth much more than your own estimate.

Old or ugly pieces of furniture can be given a new lease of life when they are decorated with a motif such as this one.

Preparation of the piece

A piece of furniture that you already have, does not always need to be stripped of paint and varnish to receive a face lift. A good sanding over with fine sandpaper, followed by a cleaning wash, should be enough to key in the decorative paintwork.

If the surface is varnished, use methylated spirits on a clean cloth for the wash.

If the surface is painted, sand first and wash over with a solution of sugar soap and water, or use a cloth soaked in white spirits.

A laminated surface simply needs a wipe over with a mild detergent and hot water.

The piece from the junk shop can be given the same preparatory treatment, but first check that it is free of woodworm, that all the joints are firm and that the veneer, if any, is not lifting off the base-wood.

Planning the work

Regard the decoration of the piece as an extension of your own artistic ability. Psychologically, it works out better in the end for both you and the piece of furniture. If you think of it from the beginning as being a piece of junk, or something that you can throw away if you make a mistake, your work will reflect this attitude and the result will be poor.

Study the shape and form of the piece before starting work. Proportions should be viewed sympathetically before you decide on the style of decoration. Keep a balance between what the piece is saying and what you want to do with it.

Keeping your attitude feline, in the sense that once you have made up your mind there will be no stopping you, choose the background paint medium and colour. Listed below are different paints, their approximate drying times, the number of coats necessary, and the mediums that can be used on them for the decorative paintwork.

	Oil-based paint		
	Number of hours	Number of coats	
Undercoat	4–6	3	artists' oil colours
Eggshell	8–16	2	all oil-based glazes
Enamel	6	2	poor man's gold
Flat oil	4–6	2	acrylic paints
Gloss	8–12	2	cellulose car spray
Japan lacquer	4–6	2	
Metal primer	6	1	
Wood stains	8–12	1–2	
	Water-based paint		
Trade emulsion	1–4	2	all water-based paints
Vinyl emulsion	2–4	2	cellulose car spray
Vinyl silk	2–4	2	
Gesso	24	5–7	gesso will take oil-based paint if it is sealed with a light shellac
Acrylics	1	1–3	
Wood stains	8–12	1–2	
Cellulose	10 mins–1 hr	2–5	oil glazes, Japan lacquer, enamels, poor man's gold

Opposite *A classical, black base-coat used on a 1930s chest-of-drawers is given a Chinese golden trellis finish. Drawer handles have been gilded and distressed. Mother-of-pearl slithers add a luminous quality to flowers, foliage and birds painted in sections on the front and sides of the chest.*

Cellulose paints

Cellulose has the fastest drying time and gives a very fine surface finish. There is a vast range of colours to choose from, including metallic ones. Cellulose red primer is an excellent base for simulating red Chinese lacquer. The actual spraying should be done in a well-ventilated room. The garden-shed could double-up as a studio, but open the windows or door while spraying. Three or four coats are enough to build up a base colour. Then try one of the following methods.

On a plain background, stencilwork using acrylics or bronze powders, as in poor man's gold, can be completed in half a day. Cellulose spray can be used in stencilwork too, but be extra careful that the spray does not spread over the stencil card.

Cracklure and porphyry look mellow and attractive on medium to pale surfaces. On darker base colours, they add richness and depth.

Marbling and rag-rolling can be used on large surfaces to greater effect than on smaller areas, but the price of cellulose car spray usually prevents its being used with these techniques on a grand scale. Stippling or dragging would be more appropriate and quicker.

Tortoise-shell, malachite, and lapis lazuli in the water-based method will give no problems, but make sure you have the correct base colour.

Varnish for cellulose Polyurethane varnish covers just about everything. The resilient surface is impervious to stains, moisture and heat. The drawback is that there is no solvent for it once it has been applied. Removal of the varnish will completely destroy your work. Used over pale pastels, its yellow quality tends to turn them into shadows of their former selves, so do allow for this, especially with tints of blue.

If you are using a polyurethane varnish over cellulose paint you cannot re-spray cellulose over it again as this will cause bubbling and cracking over the entire surface.

Oil-based paints

The average drying time for oil-based paints is approximately six to eight hours. Overnight drying is best for most paint that will be taking a decorative finish. Then your high energy level in the morning can be employed for the enjoyable part of furniture transformation. Good preparation forms nine-tenths of success so do not skimp. Numerous undercoats, each followed by sandpapering until you feel your arm will drop off, is time-consuming and hard work but you can console yourself with the thought that the better the finish, the higher the praise. The possibilities when using oil paints are endless. Glazes galore, in hundreds of combinations, can be set off with marble and tortoise-shell veneer, or can simply be lined and distressed.

Water-based paints

For speed and efficiency you cannot beat modern emulsions and acrylic paint. They can be applied with brushes, sponges, cloths or rollers and dry in a matter of two or three hours. However, as decorative furniture paint, it does not stand up well to wear and tear. Because of the water content in the paint, the surface remains somewhat porous. In the case of vinyl paints this is not at once obvious, but traces of moisture on or behind the surface will weaken the binding element, eventually causing the paint to bubble or peel.

Opposite Ringing the changes on the same fire surround. Totally individual looks can be achieved in a very short space of time.

A fine varnish will help to seal the surface if the piece is going to be subjected to normal family use. Remember that most varnishes will discolour with age and atmospheric conditions, and a build-up of two or more coats will alter the base colour considerably.

In the past, water-based colours have been used for many styles of decorative paintwork. Those whose techniques spring to mind as outstanding are the ancient Egyptians, the Minoan civilization of Crete, the splendours of Pompei and Rome. The stencilwork of the early American settlers, although naive in a way, was employed with great care and sympathy for the piece. Venetian lacquer was produced by varnishing over water-based paints; free-flowing scrolls, swags and flowers enhanced tables, trays, bedheads and blacka-moors. The list goes on and on.

You do not have to be a wallflower when trying out water-based paints; jump in with both brushes and hands. It may sound like a slogan for a well known soft drink, but try running through this for practice: rag it drag it pencil it then stencil it line it to refine it employ it and enjoy it.

LINING-IN

Lining-in speaks for itself. Fine lines of a contrasting or toning colour are added to stress the shape and features of the piece once it has been painted. Inset borders on the top of a chest, handles, and drawer front can all be given the same treatment: a single line created by a continuous brush-stroke meeting at the corners or curving with the shape of the furniture. The cheat's way of doing it, of course, is to use a crayon but the resulting hard line has none of the appeal of a painted line.

Special long-haired brushes are produced for performing this tricky operation. It looks very easy, but it is actually quite a challenge to use a steady hand with just the right amount of pressure behind it. A guide-line to rest the metal ferrule of the brush against is a great help. A straight-edge lifted at an angle of 45° to the brush is best (fig. 32). Any oil paint can be used for lining, but a fast-drying opaque watercolour is easier to use.

With a sharp, hard lead pencil, rule lightly along the lines where you wish to apply the colour.

For straight lines using the straight-edge at an angle of 45° to the surface being painted, load the brush with colour and draw it along the pencil line. Keep the straight-edge in position until you have finished the line. The shaft of the brush should rest gently against the side of the straight-edge all the time.

If you want to paint curving lines and irregularities, try the following techniques until you find one that suits you and your work.

Cut a fine line in stencil card and stencil the irregularity. Curves can be cut easily by using a template taken directly from the piece.

If the line you are painting can be kept relatively close to the outside of the piece use your little finger and its neighbour wedged against it to steady your hand. A cloth with white spirits or water, depending on what paint you are using, comes in handy for wiping off mistakes if they occur.

Masking-tape, so long as it is secure, can take all the wobbles out of

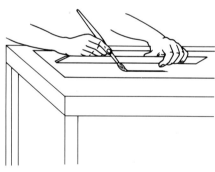

32 Lining-in.

paint of choice
long-haired sable brush
straight-edge (metal or wood)
pencil
container for paint
paper towels or rag

A Chinese design of the eighteenth century accents the back, arms and cross-bars of a 1950s chair. The gold work on this piece was executed by using a metallic gold marker-pen.

lining. It can create a slightly machine-made effect, but taking into account the time involved if you are continuously making mistakes, it is worthwhile trying it.

For the very small piece with intricate lines, waterproof drawing ink or Indian ink can be used with an ordinary fountain pen. Try a sample first to make sure the medium does not separate on the surface.

After lining the work, leave it to dry, then seal it with a clear matt or semi-matt varnish.

DISTRESSING

Words of course can be misleading, as is the term 'distressing'. The look of age on antique furniture is part and parcel of its appeal and there are various tricks of the trade for giving pieces that mellow, worn look.

Oil-glaze distressing

The stockpot of leftover oil glazes tipped into one container gives the best possible mixture for imitating the subtleties of age. Freshly mixed artists' colours in murky khaki, olive brown or dusty grey do not have the same effect. However, if it is a case of mix-on-the-day, the following recipe will give you a base to work from.

300 ml (12 fl oz) white spirits
2 teaspoons scumble glaze (see page 12)
1 tablespoon artists' oil colour mixed to one of the following colours:
Khaki: raw sienna, oxide of chromium, light red, black and white
Olive brown: yellow ochre: terre vert raw umber white
Dusty grey: raw umber, ultramarine, black white

Mix all the ingredients together.

Whether you are using old glaze or new, it is best to mix it to the colour nearest to the background colour of the piece you are painting. The thinner the glaze, the better.

Apply a fairly transparent coat of glaze with the varnish brush. Leave for two minutes.

Pounce with a sponge until you have a fine, mottled-looking surface over all.

Use a cloth to wipe off this thin glaze around the edges of doors, drawers, handles and anywhere that would naturally get more wear than the rest of the surface through constant handling or rubbing.

Dip the stencil brush into the glaze and flick the bristles over the surface. Avoid creating a regular pattern, and don't cover the whole piece. It is accepted that only the top of the piece is given this extra-fine speckle.

Using a fine-haired artists' brush dipped in white spirits, remove small spots back to the base colour. These will stand out when the

stockpot of oil glazes or newly mixed
   glaze
white spirits
varnishing brush
fine, pointed artists' brush
stencil brush
sponge
cloth or paper towels
container for glaze

The glaze can be wiped off the raised surfaces and edges of doors and drawers to give the piece a worn look.

work is viewed from a distance. Keep them few in number if you want the distressing to look good.

Wait for the glaze to dry and then varnish.

To distress the piece further, wrap a piece of wire wool or light sandpaper around one finger and, working cautiously, go over the areas that were lightened with the cloth. Some decorative artists go right back to the undercoat. However, there are no regulations or rules. You must judge how far to take this technique.

An alternative to this fine distressing is an application of a coat of dark, antique wax polish in the natural recesses. The depth and aged look take on a heavier feel, but that in itself can add character to a piece.

Water-wash distressing

This is a light wash method of distressing. It is a little difficult to handle on large surfaces. The drying time can be both a hindrance and a help.

Raw umber, thinned until it is completely transparent, is a good colour choice.

Mix the gouache or poster paint.

Wet the rag with water and wring it out; then dip it into the coloured wash.

Wipe over the piece of furniture with this fine wash, leaving the lightest possible covering. You will find the cloth leaves deposits of colour in the natural nooks and crannies that dust would have settled in over the years.

For darker areas, use the rag with a pouncing movement. This will leave irregular lines and blotches, but that is a necessary part of any distressing.

artists' gouache or poster paint
soft old rag
stencil brush
paper towels

Dip the stencil brush into the wash and flick areas of tiny spots onto the surface. The higher you hold the brush above the piece, the greater the surface area covered by the spots; the lower you hold the brush, the denser the spots become. Do watch out for spots straying too far. Distressed wallpaper or curtains may not be to your liking.

Using a damp paper towel, and taking care not to wipe off too much of this ageing over-coat, lift out the areas that would normally become worn; for example, the edges of doors, handles, and so on.

When you are happy with the effect, let the work dry. Then seal it with a matt varnish. Acrylic matt varnish is a clear, non-yellowing varnish suitable for decorative pieces, but two or three coats will be necessary if the piece is going to be used as domestic furniture. Polyurethane covers most surfaces, although the yellowing character of this varnish can greatly change pastel colours within a matter of months.

Distressing distressing

This is the other side of the coin to the gentle art of the painted finish. The list of materials reads more like the refuse from some street-gang fight: bags of nails, bicycle chains and blunt chisels. It is a shame to omit knuckle-dusters, as these would work admirably if your fist is strong enough.

The whole point of the exercise is to bash the piece of furniture about in the hope that the finished look will give the appearance of excessive wear through the ages. Manufacturers of reproduction

sandpaper
wire wool
large nails, loose in a cloth bag or old
   towel
bicycle chain
bradall (for woodworm holes)
blunt chisel
mallet
bunch of keys

furniture do not usually go this far, but the crafty furniture restorer may have to resort to these lengths to achieve harmony and balance in the piece being restored.

Knocks, bumps, scratches, woodworm holes, even rot, can all be simulated. Hours of whittling, probing and bashing can go into a single piece. You must decide how far this mild destruction should go. The list of suitable equipment is a guide, but do try to be sympathetic rather than sadistic.

APPENDICES

GLAZE QUANTITIES

It is not easy to judge the amount of glaze required
for any one job. One person's light application of paint could easily
be another's heavy-handed effort. The following quantities are on the generous side.
The leftovers can be used in the melting-pot for a soupy off-shade
that defies description but always looks good.

Area	Glaze quantity
1 Bath side-panel, or door:	½ cup – 200 ml ½ cup – ⅓ pt
2 Room: 1½ × 2 m × 2½ m ceiling 4 ft × 6 ft × 8 ft ceiling	500 ml 1 pt
3 Room: 2 m × 2½ m × 2½ m ceiling 6 ft × 8 ft × 8 ft ceiling	800 ml 1½ pt
4 Room: 2½ m × 4 m × 3 m ceiling 8 ft × 12 ft × 9 ft ceiling	1 litre 2 pt
5 Room: 3½ m × 4½ m × 3 m ceiling 10 ft × 13 ft × 9 ft ceiling	1.5 litre 2½ pt
6 Room: 4 m × 5 m × 3 m ceiling 12 ft × 15 ft × 9 ft ceiling	2 litre 3½ pt
7 Room: 5 m × 7 m × 3½ m ceiling 15 ft × 20 ft × 10 ft ceiling	3 litre 5 pt
8 Average mid-Victorian family house hall, stairs and landing:	3 litre 5 pt
9 For bookshelves and architectural details at sides of fireplaces, add an extra 150 ml (¼ pt) of glaze to the above quantity.	

VARNISHES

MATT VARNISHES

Varnishes	Manufacturer	Suitable surfaces
Artists' acrylic matt varnish	Winsor & Newton	Acrylic paint or water-based surface.
Cryla matt varnish	George Rowney	For all wall surfaces that don't receive a lot of wear and tear.
Dead matt varnish	Ratcliffs	For all oil-based glazes.
Polyurethane matt coat	Ronseal Stirling Roncraft	Yellows after a while. Suitable for heavy-duty wear and tear. All surfaces.
Artists' matt varnish	Winsor & Newton George Rowney	For small objects decorated in oil paint.
Emulsion glaze	Manders (gard)	For sealing the surface of emulsion paints and wallpapers.

SEMI-MATT VARNISHES

Fixative spray	Winsor & Newton George Rowney	All marbled papers; some porous surfaces before applying further colour.
Polyurethane satin coat	Ronseal Stirling Roncraft	For all surfaces decorated in oil-based paint and glazes.
Polyurethane eggshell	Winfield Cover Plus	For all surfaces decorated in oil-based paint and glazes.

GLOSS VARNISHES

Artists' acrylic gloss varnish	Winsor & Newton	For all acrylic paints on oil-based paint.
Cryla gloss varnish	George Rowney	For all acrylic paints on oil-based paint.
Polyurethane gloss	Ronseal Stirling Roncraft	For all heavy-duty-wear walls, furniture, etc., where a shiny finish is required.
Artists' picture varnish	Winsor & Newton George Rowney	For small objects and surfaces that don't get a lot of wear and tear.
Yacht varnish	Many manufacturers	A thick, heavy varnish for exterior use. Very yellow in colour.
Spray polyurethane	Humbrol U Spray Borden UK	Light, clear polyurethane; can be used on everything except porous surfaces.

REFERENCE GUIDE FOR DECORATIVE WORK

The best reference library in the world would only go half way to providing the number of ideas that are to be found in nature.

Artists in the past have learned to stylize natural phenomenon to the point where they are no longer recognisable, ranging from the sublime to the ridiculous. However, it is not necessary to go this far. Plant and animal forms are a joy to study. Uncomplicated outline drawings, done in the garden or local park, can start off a chain reaction of related ideas, many of which you probably never saw any potential in until you studied them a little closer. The key word, of course, is 'closer'. It is not enough to look; inspect is better; to examine microscopically reveals an enormous storehouse of possible designs. Landscapes, rock formations, clouds, the sea and the shore, are all filled with design ideas.

Man's own machinery yields many a magical cog that, turned in the hands of a decorative artist, can become a stencilled border, a silk-screen print on a scarf, or a glass painting. The reflective, sometimes distorted, images on shiny surfaces are also well worth exploiting. Sunlight and shade lend a helping hand in producing phantoms of reality; a kind of unnatural nature study. There is no need to sit befuddled when everywhere around you lie so many ideas for your work.

FURTHER READING

Barle, J., *Japanese Art and Design* (Victoria & Albert Museum, London, 1986)

Bazzi, M., *The Artist's Method And Materials*

Bishop, A. and Lord C., *The Art of Decorative Stencilling* (Thames and Hudson, London, 1976)

Cenini, C., *The Craftsman's Handbook*

Dorner, L., *The Materials of the Artist* (Harcourt, Brace and World, New York, 1934, revised edition 1962)

Garner, P., *Encyclopedia of Decorative Art 1890-1940* (Phaidon Press, 1978)

Herberts, K., Oriental Lacquer, Art and Technique (H. V. Abrahams, New York, 1963)

Jones, O., *The Grammar of Ornament* (Omega Books, Hertfordshire, England, 1986 edition)

Mayer, R., *The Artist's Handbook of Materials and Techniques* (Viking Press, New York, 1959)

Millman, M., *Trompe L'Oeil Painting, The Illusion of Reality* (Macmillan, London, 1983)

O'Neil, I., *The Art of the Painted Finish* (Morrow, New York, 1971)

Parry, J., *Graining and Marbling* (Crosby Lockwood and Sons, London, first edition, 1949, second edition, 1954)

Prisse d'Avennes, E., *The Decorative Art of Arabia* (Studio Editions, London, 1989)

Reed, K., *The Painter's Companion* (Webb Books Inc, Cambridge, Mass, 1961)

Stalker, J. and Parker, G., *A Treatise of Japanning and Varnishing* (London, 1688, new edition (Academy edition), London, 1971)

Sutherland, W., *The Grainer, Marbler And Sign Writer's Assistant* (William Atton & Co, 1854)

The Practical Home Decorating and Repairs Illustrated (Odhams, London, 1952)

Whitlock, N., *The Decorative Painters and Glaziers Guide* (Isaac Taylor Hunton, London, 1827)

Winsor and Newton, *Notes On The Composition and Permanence Of Artist Colours* (For Reckitt and Colman, Leisure Ltd, 1982)

Winsor and Newton, *Paint and Painting* (Tate Gallery Publications, London, 1982)

MANUFACTURERS AND SUPPLIERS

UNITED KINGDOM

Brodie and Middleton
68, Drury Lane, London WC2.

French enamel varnish; scenic artists' paints. Orders by post accepted.

Cornelissen, L. and Son Ltd
105, Great Russell Street, London WC1B 3RY.

Bronze powders; pigments; fabric paints; whiting; rabbit-skin granules; linen canvas; oil paints; artists' gouache. Orders by post accepted.

Green and Stone Ltd
259, Kings Road, London SW3.

Scumble glazes; varnishes; decorative artists' brushes; Dutch metal foils; artists' oil colours; fabric paint; glass paints. Orders by post accepted.

Hamilton and Co. (London) Ltd
Wealdstone, Harrow, Middlesex.

Manufacturers of decorative artists' brushes; general household paintbrushes of the best quality.

Heffer, F. A., and Co. Ltd
24 The Pavement, Clapham, London SW4.

Decorative artists' brushes of all types.

Humbrol (Borden UK) Ltd
Marfleet, Hull.

Manufacturers of non-toxic enamel paints (model-makers' enamels); polyurethane in spray canisters; Humbrol thinners.

Keep, J. T., and Sons Ltd
15 Theobalds Road, London WC1.

General decorators' sundries; large range of specialist paints; brushes; bronze powders; scumble glaze; oil paints for staining glazes; varnishes; metal, rubber, glass paints; enamel paints; flat oil paints. Orders by post accepted.

Myland, J. Ltd
80 Norwood High Street, London SE27.

French polish manufacturers. All types of varnishes.

Paperchase Products Ltd
213 Tottenham Court Road, London W1.

Stencil card; papers of all types; books of stencil designs.

Ploton, E., (Sundries), Ltd
273 Archway Road, London N6.

Artists' oil colours; metallic foils; canvasses; cracklure mixtures, ready-made; artists' varnishes; rabbit-skin granules; whiting.

Reeves Dryad Ltd
178 Kensington High Street, London W8.
Head Office: PO Box 91, Whitefriars Avenue, Wealdstone, Harrow.

Artists' oil paints; designers' gouache; fabric paints; glass paints; fabric dyes; screen-printing dyes; marbling colours; Carrahgeen moss; moss size preservative; allum crystals; oxgall; stencil paper; scalpels and blades; varnishes; papers.

Roberson and Co. Ltd 1A Hercules Street, London N7.	Artists' oil paints; canvases; varnishes; spray adhesives; bronze powders and bronze powder mediums; watercolours; drawing inks; diffuser sprays.
Rowney, G., and Co. Ltd 12 Percy Street, London W1.	Artists' oil paints; watercolours; waterproof inks; gouache; poster colour; papers; cards; varnishes.
Russell and Chapple Ltd 23 Monmouth Street, London WC2.	Canvas and calico; muslin and assorted fabrics.
Shell Shop, The 16 Manette Street, London W1.	Mother-of-pearl; Abalone shell slithers; semi-precious stones; fossil stones; real malachite.
Sterling Roncraft Chapeltown, Sheffield S30 4YP.	Polyurethane varnishes; wood stains; wood preservative; wax finishes for wood.
Wiggins Teape 34 Marshgate Lane, London E15.	Paper manufacturers and importers; suppliers in bulk of Kromekote card for producing samples and experimenting with oil glazes.

Mail Order (UK)
Papers and Paints
4 Park Walk, London SW10 0AD.

UNITED STATES

Art Essential of New York Lawrence and Jackson Street, Spring Valley, NY 10977.	Gold leaf.
Janovic Plaza 1150 Third Avenue, New York, NY 10021.	Paints and glazing mediums; solvents and varnishes; brushes.
New York Central Supply 62 Third Avenue, New York, NY 10003.	Paints and glazing mediums; solvents and varnishes; brushes.
Sepp Leaf 381 Park Avenue South, New York, NY 10016.	Gold leaf.
Weiser and Teitel 152 Avenue D 3D, New York, NY 10009.	Paints and glazing mediums; solvents and varnishes; brushes.

As paints, varnishes and brushes differ from one manufacturer to another, it is necessary for any servant of the Decorative Arts to know individual qualities when choosing materials.

Terminology changes from country to country and certain items may not even be available. It is therefore necessary to inquire from the suppliers the exact structure of the item used. Experimenting can of course be great fun but it is to be considered as very time consuming. It is much easier for the practising hand to have at its fingertips materials that work for them and not the opposite way around. If in doubt, do ask the colourman or even the manufacturer's laboratory to give you as much information as possible.

INDEX